The parts of a flower

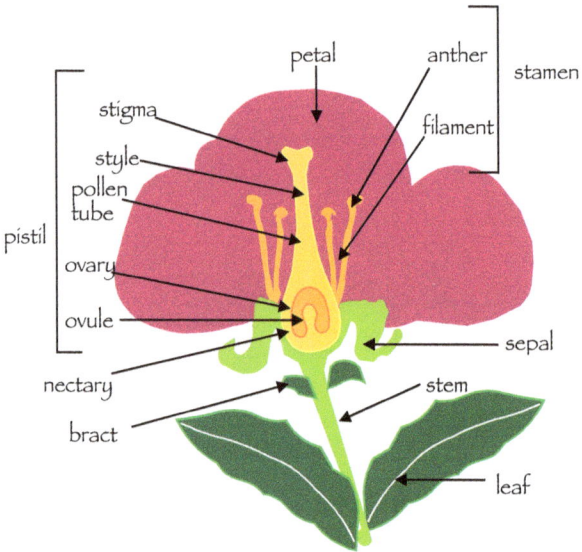

Tepals are petal or sepal-like segments that grow on some flowers, or where the sepals and petals are fused into one. Examples are the flowers of anemones, tulips, lilies, magnolias, cacti, and hellebores. They often look just like petals, but without sepals below them.

ALKANET: GREEN

LATIN NAME: Pentaglottis Sempervirens

COMMON NAMES: Alkanet; Evergreen Bugloss

BEST TIME TO SEE: April - June

FLOWER COLOUR: Blue

HEIGHT/STEM LENGTH: Up to 1m

- Alkanet is a member of the borage family, with bright sky-blue flowers, pink in bud, at the tops of stems and branches. The flower buds are covered in white hairs, and the flowers have white honey-guides and a white pentagonal ring in the centre.

- The plant is popular with bees, especially early in the season when there isn't much else to find. Orange Tip and Green-veined White butterflies, hoverflies and solitary bees also love the flowers.

- Extracts from the root can be used to make a purple or burgundy dye, with alkaline compounds used to increase the blue pigment, and acid ones turning it red again.

- The root was also used in varnishes for fine wood items such as violins.

A FASCINATING FACT

The leaves of Alkanet are used by at least two species of leaf-mining flies.

AQUILEGIA

LATIN NAME: Aquilegia vulgaris

COMMON NAMES: Columbine; Granny's Night-cap; Granny's Bonnet; Crowfoot

BEST TIME TO SEE: April - June

FLOWER COLOUR Petals & tepals; White, pink or bluish purple

HEIGHT/STEM LENGTH: to 100cm

🌿 The Columbine or Aquilegia is a tall, branching plant with large, distinctive, exotic blooms in purple, pink or blue. Some of these plants are escapes from gardens, but there are over 60 different species in this group, and they are found in the wild all over the Northern Hemisphere.

🌿 The petals were thought to look like five doves in a ring, and the name Columbine actually comes from 'columba', meaning dove. The word 'aquila' means 'eagle', referring to the shape of the top of the petals which looks like an eagle's claws.

A FASCINATING FACT

Bumblebees steal the nectar by biting into the back of the base of the petals.

A NOTE ON TOXICITY

All parts of the Columbine plant are toxic.

ANEMONE:WOOD

LATIN NAME: Anemone nemorosa

COMMON NAMES: Wind-flower; Grandmother's Nightcap; Thimbleweed

BEST TIME TO SEE: March - May

FLOWER COLOUR: Tepals - white/ pale pink; Centre- yellow, green

HEIGHT/STEM LENGTH: Up to 30cm

✻ In the wild, Wood Anemone flowers shine out in woods and hedgerows. The flowers are usually white but may be pink, lilac or blue, and often have a darker tint on the back of the tepals (petal-like segments). They never bloom earlier than March 16th, or later than April 22nd.

✻ At night, or if Spring rain threatens, the flowers will close and droop, so the rain falls on the back of the tepals, and trickles off harmlessly from the tips. Country people thought that fairies nestled in the flowers at night and for protection from the rain, after pulling the pale pink and white curtains round them.

A NOTE ON TOXICITY

All parts of the <u>fresh</u> plant are now thought to be poisonous if eaten in quantity. Dried plant parts are not poisonous.

BALSAM; HIMALAYAN

LATIN NAME: Impatiens glandulifera

COMMON NAMES: Policeman's Helmet; Gnome's Hatstand; Jewelweed

BEST TIME TO SEE: June - November

FLOWER COLOUR: Petals - pale pink & white; Central parts - pink or white

HEIGHT/STEM LENGTH: 100 - 200cm

- You will usually find this plant in ditches and near water. With its pink, orchid-like flowers, it is a beautiful but dangerously invasive species, quickly colonising canals, railway lines and rivers, choking out other plants.

- This exotic-looking plant escaped to the wild from gardens, and now grows throughout the UK. There is an ongoing discussion about whether efforts should be made to eradicate it.

- The flowers have a heavy sickly scent, and are very attractive to many insects, including bees, producing a large amount of pollen over a long season.

A FASCINATING FACT

Himalayan Balsam can throw its little seeds an amazing seven metres (23ft) from its explosive seed pods!

BEDSTRAW; HEDGE

LATIN NAME: Galium mollugo
COMMON NAMES: False Baby's Breath; Great Bedstraw
TIME TO SEE: June - September
FLOWER COLOUR: Petals - white; Central parts - greenish white
STEM LENGTH: 100 - 150cm

🌿 With its four tiny white petals, arranged in a clearly defined cross, Hedge Bedstraw stems and blossoms weave through other meadow plants. It grows best in field margins and wilder areas, forming thick mats with long spreading stems among long grasses, vetches and other early summer flowers.

🌿 Bedstraw was once used to stuff mattresses and pillows, but the name is more likely to refer to the 'Cradle herbs' found in the manger at Bethlehem.

🌿 The roots give a natural orange or red dye, when boiled. The dye will work best on natural fabrics such as cotton or linen.

A FASCINATING FACT

Bedstraws are a favourite food plant of the caterpillars of many moths, including the large, now endangered Hummingbird Hawk-moth.

BETONY

LATIN NAME: Stachys Officianalis

COMMON NAMES: Common Hedgenettle; Purple Betony; Wood Betony; Bishop's Wort

BEST TIME TO SEE: June - October

FLOWER COLOUR: Magenta

HEIGHT/STEM LENGTH: 75cm

❀ Providing a bright splash of colour late in the summer, this sturdy little perennial has stems with soft white hairs topped with bright magenta flowers held proudly on the almost leafless square stems. It grows on sunny banks and hedgerows, on heathland and other grassy places including undisturbed margins of fields.

❀ Sadly, Betony is a flower that has suffered from the catastrophic loss of meadows and the decline in woodland coppicing, so it is now less widespread.

❀ Betony was one of the great 'all-heals' of medieval herbalists. It is thought that the chemicals in betony may decrease blood pressure, and might be useful for treating headache and anxiety.

A FASCINATING FACT

It was once believed that planting the flower in churchyards provided protection against ghosts. Betony was also thought to be a remedy for drunkenness.

BILBERRY

LATIN NAME: Vaccinium myrtillus

COMMON NAMES: Whortleberry; Hurtle-berry; Whinberry; Fraughan

BEST TIME TO SEE: August - September

FLOWER COLOUR: Petals/bells - dark pink; Centre - white; Fruit blue/black

HEIGHT/STEM LENGTH: 20 - 60cm

- Bilberry plants often grow alongside Heather bushes. The rosy, dark pink flowers hang from the bushes like miniature Christmas tree decorations, and in the Autumn the red leaves contrast with the green and purple of the Heather.

- The Bilberry is related to the widely cultivated North American Blueberry, but is not the same. UK Bilberries are smaller and have many more seeds, set in red flesh.

- The juice from berries will stain your hands, clothing and faces so take care when you gather them. Birds love these dark berries and will often flock to feast on them, leaving tell-tale purple stains on walls and paths.

A FASCINATING FACT

The fruit can be used to make puddings, cakes, jams and syrups, and the juice can also be used to flavour ice cream or custards.

18

BITTERCRESS; HAIRY

LATIN NAME: Cardamine hirsuta

COMMON NAMES: Lambscress;
Landcress; Flickweed; Shotweed

TIME TO SEE: January - November

FLOWER COLOUR: White

HEIGHT/STEM LENGTH: 5 - 30cm

- This tiny plant, with small leaves and even tinier white flowers, grows abundantly in any damp, shady place.

- Bittercress is one of the first plants to flower in the early Spring. The plants grow quickly, in a 12-week cycle from seed to flowers, producing several generations in a year.

- The little pea-like seed pods explode when you touch them, and seem to be able to throw the tiny seeds some distance away from the mother plant, where they quickly germinate between rocks and in walls to make new colonies.

A FASCINATING FACT

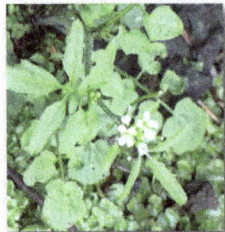

All Bittercresses are rich in vitamin C. You can eat them in salads, make them into pesto or salsa, or fry them with garlic, onion and crushed chilli for a tasty green dish.

BLUEBELL; ENGLISH

LATIN NAME: Hyacinthoides non-scriptus

COMMON NAMES: Lady's Nightcap; Granfer Griggles; Witches' Thimble

BEST TIME TO SEE: April - May

FLOWER COLOUR: Blue/white/pink

HEIGHT/STEM LENGTH: 20 - 50cm

- Half the world's Bluebells are found in the UK, and English Bluebells are threatened and protected - It is against the law to pick them or to trample their leaves and stems.

- The English Bluebell has a drooping head, with as many as 20 sweetly-scented flowers with white or cream anthers, on a stalk which droops or nods to one side. The flowers can be blue, white or rarely pink.

- You may also find the Spanish Bluebell, which has blue anthers in white or blue flowers. This flower is an escape from gardens and parks.

- The making and wearing a wreath of bluebells was once thought to compel the wearer to tell the truth.

A FASCINATING FACT

In the Middle Ages Bluebell root sap was used to glue feathers to arrows.

BLACKBERRY

LATIN NAME: Rubis fruticosis

COMMON NAMES: Black Heg; Blegs; Bramble

TIME TO SEE: August - September

FLOWER COLOUR: Pale/dark pink

STEM LENGTH: up to 4m

🌺 Blackberry bushes grow in hedgerows and field margins across every country in the UK, producing flowers with fragile pink petals, and red fruit, which turns black as it ripens.

🌺 The black fruit is not really a berry, but an 'aggregate fruit', made up of many 'drupelets', each containing its own little brown seed. The fruits yield a blue dye, and fibres from the stems have been used to make string.

🌺 Bramble flowers are a food source for honey bees, bumblebees and other wild animals, especially deer. Ripe berries are eaten and seeds dispersed by mammals such as the wood mouse, fox and badger. Blackberry bushes also provide a home for small animals, including grass snakes.

A FASCINATING FACT

Some people believe that after 30th September, Blackberries left on the bushes belong to the Devil - check your calendar before you go blackberrying late in the year!

BROOM

LATIN NAME: Cytisus scoparius

COMMON NAMES: Scotch Broom; Scot's Broom

BEST TIME TO SEE: April - August

FLOWER COLOUR: Yellow; Centre -yellow or white

HEIGHT/STEM LENGTH: up to 2.5m

🌼 Broom is a member of the pea family, similar to Gorse, but with no prickles, just masses of vanilla scented, pale or deeper yellow flowers on long, stiff stems above mounds of bright green leaves. Wild bees and particularly Bumblebees love it.

🌼 Broom has been used for many years to make brooms, baskets, and even to strengthen fences or thatch houses. The wood from mature plants can produce a beautifully veined veneer for furniture and the leaves make a green dye for natural clothing fabrics such as cotton or linen.

🌼 During the summer, the hairy, black seed pods of Broom explode in the sun, producing a loud cracking sound and spreading their seeds.

A FASCINATING FACT

The smell of broom was said to tame wild horses and dogs.

A NOTE ON TOXICITY

All parts of the Broom plant are toxic to humans and animals if eaten.

BUGLE

LATIN NAME: Ajuga reptans

COMMON NAMES: Blue Bugle; Carpet Bugleweed; St. Lawrence Plant

BEST TIME TO SEE: April - July

FLOWER COLOUR: Purple/blue with white markings

HEIGHT/STEM LENGTH: 10 - 30cm

🌿 Bugle has deep purple or blue flower spikes, standing proudly above the rosettes of green, hairy, purplish leaves, decorated with small, purple flowers shaped like little ladies in purple petticoats. Faint stripes run down the petals to lead a variety of visiting insects to the nectar. These include many butterflies. Carder Bees also feed on its nectar, and Bugle is much loved by bumblebees.

🌿 Bugle is sometimes confused with Selfheal, however on this plant the flowers are arranged more tightly at the top of the stem. 'Reptans' in its Latin name is from 'creeping or crawling'.

🌿 Bugle has a long medicinal history. The herb is gathered and dried in May and June when the leaves are young and at their best.

A FASCINATING FACT

The roots of Bugle plants will produce a natural black dye which can be used for organic fabrics, such as cotton or linen.

BURNET: GREAT

LATIN NAME: Sanguisorba officinalis

COMMON NAMES: Bloodwort; Common Burnet; Salad Burnet; Italian Burnet; Italian Pimpernel

BEST TIME TO SEE: June - September

FLOWER COLOUR: Deep crimson

HEIGHT/STEM LENGTH: 1.2m

🌾 The egg-shaped, crimson flower heads of Great Burnet make this plant look like a bunch of lollipops! Every dark red head contains many tiny flowers, and each of these can produce many seeds.

🌾 A surprising member of the rose family, Great Burnet is a perennial and can survive harsh conditions for decades due to its extensive and deep root system. It can be found on undisturbed pasture and floodplain meadows - declining habitats which are under serious threat.

🌾 Great Burnet is an important food plant for many insects, in particular the European Large Blue butterfly.

🌾 Herbalists used the herb to stop bleeding.

A FASCINATING FACT

The crimson heads of Great Burnet were once used in Cumbria to make wine.

BUTTERBUR

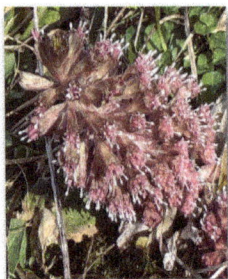

LATIN NAME: Petasites hybridus

COMMON NAMES: Blatterdock; Bog Rhubarb; Bogshorns; Butterdock; Capdockin; Flapperdock; Langwort; Umbrella Plant

BEST TIME TO SEE: March - May

FLOWER COLOUR: Pink

HEIGHT/STEM LENGTH: 10-40cm

🌿 Fond of moist ground, this pink, tasseled, vanilla smelling wildflower can often be found carpeting riversides and damp ditches, and the flowers usually appear before the leaves.

🌿 Each flower spike consists of around 15 to 25 pink flower heads, but its name derives from its large, heart-shaped leaves that were used to wrap butter in the past to keep it cool in summer.

🌿 The leaves grow huge, eventually looking rather like rhubarb - as a result this flower is also called Bog Rhubarb. It is very invasive forming huge clumps.

🌿 Butterbur is very popular with bees and other pollinators, as it is a great source of nectar early in the year, when wildflowers are sparse.

A FASCINATING FACT

The name is from the Greek 'petasos', meaning a 'broad-brimmed felt hat' after the enormous leaves.

BUTTERCUP

LATIN NAME: Ranunculacae.

SOME COMMON NAMES: Gold Cup;
Bachelor's Buttons; Meadowbloom

BEST TIME TO SEE: May - June

FLOWER COLOUR: Golden yellow;
Central parts - yellow/green

HEIGHT/STEM LENGTH: 10 - 60cm

Buttercups stand above the new grasses, and the golden flood of flowers, pouring down a natural hay meadow is one of the most beautiful sights of the early Summer countryside. Three main Buttercup varieties flower in upland meadows - the tall Meadow Buttercup , the lush and greener Creeping Buttercup, and the less common Bulbous Buttercup. They often grow together and are difficult to tell apart.

Country people believed Buttercups gave butter its colour, and children still hold a flower under a friend's chin to see if they 'like butter'.

A FASCINATING FACT

Buttercups taste so horrible - even cows won't eat them!

A NOTE ON TOXICITY

Buttercups are not edible, but they are not classed as poisonous either.

CATSEAR

LATIN NAME: Hypochaeris radicata

COMMON NAMES: False Dandelion;
Hawkweed; Rooted Catsear

BEST TIME TO SEE: May - June

FLOWER COLOUR: Yellow with
greenish backs to petals

HEIGHT/STEM LENGTH: 20 - 4cm

🌼 The rosettes of Catsear leaves are toothed like Common Dandelions, but unlike Dandelions, the flowers, buds, stems and leaves are hairy, with smaller yellow petals, toothed at the ends. These 'faux Dandelions' flower in thousands on sunny slopes of many hay meadows and footpath verges.

🌼 Members of the Dandelion family all attract insects, but Catsear flowers are special favourites of hoverflies and smaller insects, particularly in Spring when other flowers with higher nectar content to tempt the bees.

A FASCINATING FACT

The whole plant - fresh leaves, petals, roots and flower buds can be eaten. The leaves are bland in taste but can be eaten raw in salads, steamed, or used in stir-fries. The petals make a bright garnish for salads.

CELANDINE: LESSER

LATIN NAME: Ranunculus ficaria

COMMON NAMES: Spring Messenger; Butter & Cheese; Brighteye

BEST TIME TO SEE: March - April

FLOWER COLOUR: Shiny yellow; Centre - yellow and green

HEIGHT/STEM LENGTH: 25cm

🌱 The Celandines you will see growing wild in England are probably Lesser Celandines, the most common of this species. With their shiny yellow petals and heart-shaped leaves, they grow in moist corners of fields and damp, shady ditches near a reliable source of water. Celandines are one of the few plants that are able to carpet the ground in the shade beneath walls and trees.

🌱 In the language of flowers, the Celandine represents 'joy to come', and its glossy golden flowers herald the Spring in shining yellowness.

A FASCINATING FACT

The flowers of Celandines do not open before 9 a.m. and by 5 p.m. they are closed up tight again for the coming night.

38

CLEAVERS

LATIN NAME: Galium aparine

COMMON NAMES: Goosegrass;
Stickyweed; Everlasting Friendship

BEST TIME TO SEE: March onwards

FLOWER COLOUR: White; Central parts
-greeny white

STEM LENGTH: 300cm or more

🌿 The tiny, white, star-shaped flowers of Cleavers are easy to miss, growing in groups at the end of the square-sectioned straggling stems. The most noticeable parts of the plant are the round seed heads, which turn brown as they ripen. One plant can contain between 300 and 400 seeds, so it is quick to colonise new ground.

🌿 The seeds and stems of Cleavers are best known for their irritating habit of attaching themselves to clothing, particularly socks and jumper sleeves. The sticky seeds are covered in curved hooks that give such common names as Stickyweed.

🌿 The roots can produce a permanent red dye.

A FASCINATING FACT

Geese love to eat this plant, giving it another country name - 'Goosegrass'. The plants were gathered to feed farmyard geese.

CLOVER: RED

LATIN NAME: Trifolium pratense
COMMON NAMES: Beebread; Cow Grass; Honeystalks; Suckbottles
BEST TIME TO SEE: May – August
FLOWER COLOUR: Pale to deep reddish pink
HEIGHT: 10 – 60cm

🌺 The deep red flowers of Red Clover stud the grasses of summer hay meadows, growing in big clumps at the edges of fields, and scattered among the other flowers where grasses are more abundant. Red clover has signature white patches on its three-lobed leaves, which often grow into huge mounds.

🌺 All Clovers are known for attracting many varieties of bees, particularly honey bees and bumblebees, and they are a good source for delicious clover honey, as the nectar is rich in natural sugars.

🌺 Nectar derived from Clover flowers during late spring and summer gives a uniquely rich, strong flavour to honey collected from this honey-flavoured plant.

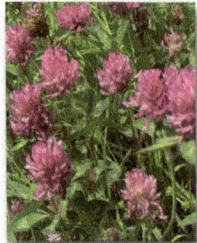

A FASCINATING FACT

All parts of the Clover, and particularly their three part leaves are thought to bring good luck. Look for a four leaved clover for extra luck!

CLOVER: WHITE

LATIN NAME: Trifolium repens

SOME COMMON NAMES: Dutch Clover; Ladino Clover; Ladino

BEST TIME TO SEE: May - September

FLOWER COLOUR: White, with pinkish ends to flowers

STEM LENGTH: up to 50cm

🌿 White Clover, with its cones of white flower petals and short stems, tends to grow at the edges of fields and on grassy footpaths, in places where the grass is shorter and land is drier. Its Latin name 'repens' means creeping, and unlike Red Clover, which spreads through seeds, White Clover spreads through long, rooting stems, forming dense mats.

🌿 White Clover is just as attractive to bees as the red variety, but it is the bumblebees that come to the White Clover. Its longer flowering season may make it as vital to pollinators as Red Clover.

A FASCINATING FACT

White Clover leaves are the inspiration for the four-leaved symbol known as the Shamrock, although there is no agreement on which is the 'real' Shamrock plant.

Look for four-leaved clover leaves on this smaller plant.

COLTSFOOT

LATIN NAME: Tussilago farfara

COMMON NAMES: Tash Plant; Ass's Foot; Bull's Foot; Coughwort; Foal's Foot; Foalswort; Horse Foot; Dishylaggie; Cleats

BEST TIME TO SEE: March - April

FLOWER COLOUR: Yellow

HEIGHT/STEM LENGTH: 10-30cm

- Coltsfoot is a flower in the daisy family that has long been cultivated for its medicinal properties. It grows in a range of habitats on open or disturbed ground, including arable land, waste land, shingle and scree, where there is poor drainage.

- The flowers, which resemble dandelions, have scale-leaves on the long stems in early spring. These leaves, appearing after the flowers have set seed, wither and die in the early summer.

- Coltsfoot is used as a food plant by the caterpillars of some butterfly species. Providing early sources of pollen and nectar It is a favourite of honeybees.

- As a herbal tea, it is said to treat respiratory infections, sore throats, gout, flu, and fever.

A FASCINATING FACT

Tussilago' is derived from the Latin 'tussis' (cough), and 'ago', (to act on or affect).

CORNCOCKLE

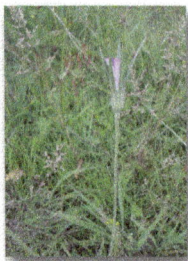

LATIN NAME: Agrostemma githago
COMMON NAMES: Cockerel; Bastard Nigella; Corn Pink; Popple; Robin Hood
BEST TIME TO SEE: May - September
FLOWER COLOUR: Bright pink with pale pink/white centre
HEIGHT/STEM LENGTH: 30 - 100cm

🌿 The Corncockle flower is unmistakeable, with its five bright magenta petals, striped to attract the bees to its pale centre. It stands proud above the grasses on a straight, hairy stem. It is now seen as very rare, and critically endangered in the wild, although its seeds sometimes come to the surface and flower after land has been disturbed, but these will not produce seed.

🌿 You may also see Corncockle flowering in conservation meadows, sown as part of a meadow seed mixture to establish new meadows.

A FASCINATING FACT

In the past, the plant was eradicated by selective weedkiller, as it was harvested with corn and mistakenly included in bread flour.

A NOTE ON TOXICITY

All parts of the plant contain toxins. When in doubt, don't eat it!

COW PARSLEY

LATIN NAME: Anthriscus sylvestris

COMMON NAMES: Queen Anne's Lace, Mother Die; Mummy Die

BEST TIME TO SEE: May - June

FLOWER COLOUR: White

HEIGHT/STEM LENGTH: Up to 1m

- One of several common members of the carrot family, this is the most abundant, and the earliest-flowering of the umbellifers. The umbrella-like clusters of white, frothy flowers of cow parsley are a familiar sight along roadsides, hedgerows and woodland edges, decorating these with masses of frothy, white flowers. Cow parsley is a favourite flower of many pollinators

- When crushed between the fingers, the leaves produce a strong, aniseed-like scent.

- The hollow stems make good pea shooters, best when they are dry at the end of summer!

A FASCINATING FACT

In some areas the plant is called 'Mummy Die', which was thought to be a warning to children not to eat it in case they eat one of its poisonous cousins.

A NOTE ON TOXICITY

Young leaves of the plant are edible, but Cow Parsley has many poisonous relatives, so it is best left uneaten!

COWSLIP

LATIN NAME: Primula veris

COMMON NAMES: Freckled Face, Golden Drops, Bunch of Keys, Fairies' Flower, Lady's Fingers, Long Legs and Milk Maidens

BEST TIME TO SEE: April - May

FLOWER COLOUR: Yellow

HEIGHT/STEM LENGTH: Up to 25cm

🌱 The Cowslip is one of the best known spring flowers. The cup-shaped, yellow blooms grow in nodding clusters on tall stalks, and the leaves are oval with wrinkled edges similar to the Primrose.

🌱 Cowslips were once as common as Buttercups. However, they suffered a decline between 1930 and 1980, due to the loss of the grasslands where they grow. These are now showing signs of recovery and the flower has begun to return to unsprayed verges and the banks of new roads.

🌱 The scent of Cowslips is not dissimilar to that of an apricot. Tea made from the flowers is found to be good for insomnia, headaches and nervous tension, and the scented flowers also make delicious wines.

A FASCINATING FACT

Cowslip allegedly means cowpat! Our ancestors noted that Cowslips tended to flower where a cow had 'slipped'.

CRANESBILL: MEADOW

LATIN NAME: Geranium pratense

COMMON NAMES: Jingling Johnny, Blue Basins, Gipsy, Grace of God; Loving Andrews

BEST TIME TO SEE: June - September

FLOWER COLOUR: Blue/Purple

HEIGHT/STEM LENGTH: Up to 75cm

- The large, purple flowers of Meadow Cranesbill turn into pointed, bill-like seed pods that give the plant its common name. The clump-forming perennial has lobed leaves that are deeply divided. In Autumn the leaves turn deep red.

- Meadow Cranesbill is a favourite of many species of bee, including Buff-tailed and Red-tailed Bumblebees, and of Honeybees, which will continue to feed in the cups of the delicate blue flowers even in heavy rain.

- With astringent, styptic (blood staunching), and antiseptic medical properties, Meadow Cranesbill and its close relatives were used to treat a range of diseases including cholera, diarrhoea, dysentery, and to treat nosebleeds, ulcers and haemorrhoids and to staunch bleeding wounds.

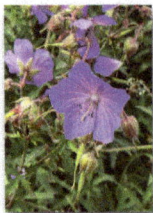

A FASCINATING FACT

Strangely for such a lovely flower, in the Language of Flowers the Meadow Cranesbill symbolises envy.

DAISY: COMMON

LATIN NAME: Bellis perennis

COMMON NAMES: Bairnswort; Day's Eye; Priest's Collar; Moonflower

BEST TIME TO SEE: Early spring

FLOWER COLOUR: Outer petals white, often with pink backs; Central florets – yellow

HEIGHT/STEM LENGTH: 3 - 12cm

🌼 Daisies produce their bright white flowers with yellow centres in the fields and under hedges before the grasses and other flowers block out the light. Later in the year, they are usually found at the edges of fields and on bridle paths, verges, ditches or under trees, where the light is brighter. They flower all year round, even in the winter, and are among the first to flower in Spring.

🌼 The Common Daisy may have been named from its original country name of 'Day's-eye' because it opens in the morning and closes at night.

A FASCINATING FACT

This charming, but often overlooked little flower was also thought to have the power to protect against lightning, but I'm not sure how you should use it!

DAISY: OX-EYE

LATIN NAME: Leucanthemum vulgare
COMMON NAMES: Moon Daisy; Dog
Daisy; Horse Daisy; Poverty-weed
BEST TIME TO SEE: June - August
FLOWER COLOUR: White; Central
florets yellow or orange
STEM LENGTH: 20 - 75cm

🌾 The big, white Ox-eye Daisies are familiar to us all, as they flower on roadside and motorway verges across the UK, in clouds of white during the early Summer. The feathery leaves disappear after flowering, but a plant can produce up to 26,000 seeds, and these are blown along roads by cars, and into fields by winds and visiting cows, so colonisation can be swift!

🌾 The childhood game of 'He loves me; he loves me not', played while picking the petals off a daisy one by one, is thought to have used the Ox-eye Daisy, not the Field Daisy, as they were much easier to handle, and grew in all cornfields.

A FASCINATING FACT

Marinated in vinegar, the unopened flower buds can be used just like capers to spice up meats and salads.

58

DANDELION

LATIN NAME: Taraxacum officinale

COMMON NAMES: Piss-en-lit; Clock Flower; Lion's Tooth; Telltime

BEST TIME TO SEE: March - May

FLOWER COLOUR: Yellow; Central parts yellow

HEIGHT/STEM LENGTH: up to 20cm

- Bright yellow Dandelions grow everywhere in fields, gardens, natural pasture, roadside banks, walls and hedgerows. The golden flowers, closing in rain or after sunset, echo the Spring sunshine, and provide food for insects of all kinds. The round, fluffy seed heads attract many species of birds, particularly Goldfinches.

- An old wives' tale says picking Dandelion flowers will make children wet the bed. This warning may be true, as the milk-white sap does contain a diuretic. However, the staining from Dandelion sap was a more likely reason for discouraging the picking of these tempting flowers!

A FASCINATING FACT

Traditionally, Dandelions were thought to represent the universe - the <u>sun</u> (the flower), the <u>moon</u> (the dandelion clock) and the <u>stars</u> (the floating seeds on their airy parachutes).

DEADNETTLE/ARCHANGEL

LATIN NAME: Lamium purpureum/
Lamium galeobdolon
SOME COMMON NAMES: Purple Dead-
Nettle; Purple Archangel
BEST TIME TO SEE: March - November
FLOWER COLOUR: Purple, White or
Yellow (Archangel)
HEIGHT/STEM LENGTH: To 30cm

🌸 Like yellow archangel, and other members of the dead-nettle family, Purple Deadnettle doesn't have stinging leaves. The name is from the Greek 'lamia' meaning 'devouring monster', as the helmet shape of the flower looks like open jaws.

🌸 Many different species of long-tongued insects visit the flowers of dead-nettles, including the Red Mason Bee and bumblebees. The caterpillars of Garden Tiger, White Ermine and Angle Shades Moth feed on the leaves.

🌸 In traditional medicine, dried leaves have been used as a poultice to stem bleeding, and fresh bruised leaves have been applied to external wounds and cuts. The leaves are also made into herbal tea.

A FASCINATING FACT

The tops and leaves are edible in salads, and the nectar makes the flowers taste sweet.

DOCK: BROAD-LEAVED

LATIN NAME: Rumex obtusifolius

COMMON NAMES: Butter Dock; Cushy-cows; Bluntleaf Dock; Dockleaf

BEST TIME TO SEE: June - August

FLOWER COLOUR: No petals; Sepals - green and red

HEIGHT/STEM LENGTH: 15 - 120cm

🌾 The Broad-leaved Dock is a tough-leaved, tall plant, with spires of green flowers that ripen to rose, then to rusty brown seeds, towering over the hay grasses. The leaves turn orange, gold and red as winter approaches, and the stems often survive through winter frosts and snows.

🌾 Dock plants grow quickly and even a small piece of root left in the ground will soon grow into a new plant. Each plant also produces thousands of seeds on its tall red spires, and these blow around to sprout quickly as soon as the hay crop has been harvested.

A FASCINATING FACT

The leaves are a traditional remedy for the pain of nettle stings, but milk, soap or baking soda will do just as well as a dock leaf, to soothe the stings.

ENCHANTER'S NIGHTSHADE

LATIN NAME: Circaea lutetiana

SOME COMMON NAMES: Sorcerer of Paris; Witch's Grass; Paris Nightshade

BEST TIME TO SEE: June - July

FLOWER COLOUR: White and pale pink

HEIGHT/STEM LENGTH: 20 - 60cm

🌿 Enchanter's Nightshade produces small red buds and little white flowers like tiny butterflies, around stamens like fairy pins. It blooms in the shade of hedgerows, growing quietly among the grasses and leaves.

🌿 It is an almost invisible flower, easy to overlook, but its romantic name is a bit of a sham, as it has no magical powers or any relation to real Nightshades which <u>are</u> poisonous.

🌿 Enchanter's Nightshade produces small, sticky brown seed heads, which catch in animal fur, later bitten or scratched off to grow far away in new places.

A FASCINATING FACT

The name of this plant shows its link with witches who were thought to use it to enslave victims, or for their own shape-shifting abilities.

FERNS

LATIN NAME: Polypodiopsida family
COMMON NAMES: Each has its own common name
BEST TIME TO SEE: Summer/Autumn
FLOWER COLOUR: Petals - none; Fruiting spores form on back of leaves
HEIGHT/STEM LENGTH: 10 - 150cm depending on species

🌿 There are more than 10,500 fern species, growing in the dry stone walls and hedgerows of upland areas.

🌿 Ferns are an ancient group of plants that do not have flowers or seeds. They spread by producing brown spores on the backs of their fronds, and these are blown away by the wind.

🌿 Look for fern fronds as they uncurl in Spring, and little ferns growing near water, trailing their fronds in the streams, greenly decorating troughs and bridges. These tiny jewels are often missed in our search for more highly coloured flowers.

A FASCINATING FACT

The roots of some ferns are strong enough to undermine stone walls.

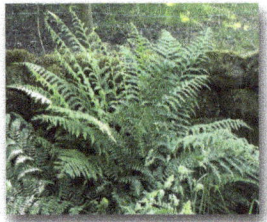

A NOTE ON TOXICITY

Bracken (a common fern species)has recently been found to be unsafe to eat.

FEVERFEW

LATIN NAME: Tanacetum parthenium
COMMON NAMES: Bachelor's Buttons; Flirtwort; Featherfoil
BEST TIME TO SEE: July - August
FLOWER COLOUR: Outer ray petals white; Central florets - yellow
HEIGHT/STEM LENGTH: 20 - 70cm

- Feverfew has white, daisy-like flowers, finely cut leaves, and an unpleasant smell, reminiscent of camphor. It is very common in some fields, but not so well-known at higher altitudes. Its strange smell is one of its major attributes, as it attracts a wide range of insects, particularly flies and hoverflies. Bees will avoid the plant, perhaps they don't like the smell!

- The plant is used in herbal medicine to treat fever, migraine headaches, stomach and tooth pain, rheumatoid arthritis, insect bites, and psoriasis.

A FASCINATING FACT

Feverfew was once planted round homes to ward off disease and purify the air before people had made the link between good hygiene and human health.

FORGET-ME-NOT: FIELD

LATIN NAME: Myosotis sylvaticus

COMMON NAMES: Love-Me; Mouse-Ear; Scorpion Grass; Snake Grass

BEST TIME TO SEE: April - May

FLOWER COLOUR: Blue or pink; Centre white and yellow

HEIGHT/STEM LENGTH: 15 - 40cm

- This charming little plant has dainty blue, pink and white flowers, with startling yellow centres. Forget-me-nots will often establish big clumps in shady ditches and on sunny banks where the soil is damp and rich.

- Stories about the Forget-me-not's name include one that, at the original naming of flowers, it was so small it was almost forgotten, and cried out 'Forget-me-not!'.

- There are also sad stories of lovers drowning or leaving their girlfriends with the flowers as a talisman for remembrance.

- The Alzheimer's Society has adopted the Forget-me-not as a symbol for their fund raising.

A FASCINATING FACT

There are some references to Forget-me-not juice being used to harden steel - but I have no details of how to do this!

72

FORGET-ME-NOT: CHANGING

LATIN NAME: Myosotis discolor

COMMON NAMES: Yellow or Blue Scorpion Grass; Scorpion Weed

BEST TIME TO SEE: April - June

FLOWER COLOUR: Blue, pink, white; Centre - white

HEIGHT/STEM LENGTH: 18 - 25cm

🌿 Changing Forget-me-not is a tiny, but fascinating plant, hidden among the field grasses. The flowers emerge as a tight little spiral of hairy buds, with flowers that change colour as they uncurl from white to blue, then pink and even violet. No-one really knows why this happens, but the plant may be sending messages to insects to tell them which of the many tiny flowers still contain nectar.

🌿 Each flower has five sepals, five petals fused into a single tube, and five tiny stamens in a little cluster at the top of a thin, hairy stalk.

A FASCINATING FACT

Changing Forget-me-not grows and flowers almost invisible in the tall grasses and late Spring flowers of meadows, often escaping our notice entirely.

FOXGLOVE

LATIN NAME: Digitalis purpurea

COMMON NAMES: Witches' Gloves; Fairy Caps; Fairy Thimbles

BEST TIME TO SEE: May – July

FLOWER COLOUR: Bells - pale to dark pink and white, or white; Centre - white

HEIGHT/STEM LENGTH: up to 200cm

The tall magenta spires of the wild Foxglove grace fields, moorlands and hedgerows at the end of Spring and through the early Summer. Whole sloping hillside field banks are often thronged with these stately flowers, and others stand still and straight in the shade of woodlands, ditches and hedgerows.

The flowers of the wild Foxglove are almost always dark pink, with rare examples in paler pink or white. All colours have spotted throats inside each flower, leading the bees deep into the blooms for nectar. Bumblebees will often struggle to get into the flowers, wriggling even more on the way out!

A FASCINATING FACT

A single Foxglove flower will just fit your finger, or a fairy's!

A NOTE ON TOXICITY

All parts of the Foxglove plant are poisonous. Just look at their beauty, and leave them for others to enjoy!

GARLIC MUSTARD

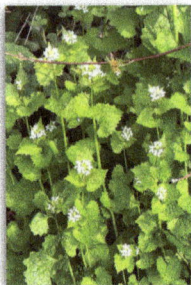

LATIN NAME: Alliaria petiolata

SOME COMMON NAMES: Jack by the Hedge; Garlic Root; Hedge Garlic; Sauce-Alone; Jack-in-the-Bush; Penny Hedge; Poor Man's Mustard

BEST TIME TO SEE: March - April

FLOWER COLOUR: White

HEIGHT/STEM LENGTH: Up to 1m

🌿 Wild Garlic, or garlic mustard is a biennial plant, taking two years to complete its lifecycle. It grows young leaves in its first season, which it keeps over winter, then flowers in the Spring of its second year, sometimes carpeting whole woodlands with starry flowers.

🌿 The small white flowers have four petals in the shape of a cross and grow in clusters at the ends of the stems. They have a rather unpleasant aroma which attracts midges and hoverflies. When crushed the leaves smell of garlic.

🌿 Roots, leaves and flowers of the plant can be eaten in salads, as pesto, or a cheese sandwich!

A FASCINATING FACT

69 insect herbivores and seven fungi are associated with garlic mustard. The most important groups of natural enemies associated with the plant are weevils, leaf beetles, butterflies and caterpillars.

78

GOATSBEARD

LATIN NAME: Tragopon pratensis

COMMON NAMES: Common Salsify; Noon Flower; Wild Oysterplant; Yellow Salsify; Yellow Goat's Beard; Meadow Goat's Beard

BEST TIME TO SEE: June - September

FLOWER COLOUR: Yellow

HEIGHT/STEM LENGTH: Up to 1m

🌿 Goatsbeard is also called 'Jack go to Bed at Noon' because the flower opens very early in the morning (it is only visible before noon). The large flower-head opens and twists slightly towards the sun each morning, and in the early afternoon, the flower-head closes again.

🌿 Once the flower-head has finished blooming, the bracts close up around the fertilised flowers, completely hiding them from view.

🌿 Later the plant forms a globe-shaped, plumed seed head that resembles that of the dandelion, but is distinctly larger (up to 10 cm) and even more beautiful as it stands in limestone meadows, among Oxeye daisies, Knapweed, and Scabious.

A FASCINATING FACT

The roots of this plant were once dug up and stored over winter to eat as a vegetable, and the young shoots were boiled and eaten like asparagus.

GORSE

LATIN NAME: Ulex europaeus

COMMON NAMES: Furze; Fingers-and-thumbs; Honey-bottle; Whin

BEST TIME TO SEE: April - May

FLOWER COLOUR: Bright yellow; Centre yellow

HEIGHT/STEM LENGTH: up to 3m

- Gorse grows in prickly piles on the edges of fields and on moorland, invading meadows if not kept in check. It provides shelter for many species of birds, including bright Yellowhammers and Stonechats finding shelter in its dense thickets.

- When Gorse blooms, it is a late Spring joy, with a bright yellowness of flowers, typical of the Pea family, and vanilla or coconut scent, making you forgive its spiky nature during the rest of the year. Gorse fruits are long brown pods, which pop open on sunny days, throwing out shiny black seeds, said to repel fleas and mice.

- The thick stems of Gorse were used for walking sticks and for strengthening fences.

A FASCINATING FACT

The flowers were used to make Gorse wine, a sweet cordial, and to flavour ice-cream and jelly.

HAREBELL

LATIN NAME: Campanula rotundifolia
COMMON NAMES: Dead Man's Bells; Bluebells of Scotland
BEST TIME TO SEE: July - September
FLOWER COLOUR: Pale blue; Centre - white
HEIGHT/STEM LENGTH: 15 - 30cm

〰 With its papery blue petals and delicate appearance, you might think the harebell a fragile wild flower. In fact, it's very tough and resilient. The harebell is a wild flower of dry, open places and they are able to grow in the most exposed places, such as walls, railway bridges, rocky cliffs and windswept hedgerows, where their blue bells wave from wire-thin stalks above little green leaflets. Tiny seeds, wind blown, soon invade other fields to start new colonies.

〰 Harebells flower at the end of the summer, and are often found in fields where cattle roam to eat up the remains of the hay crop. Lazing around in the late summer sun, these great animals might present a problem for such fragile flowers, but they seem to co-exist without any damage.

A FASCINATING FACT

The young leaves are edible, but these little flowers are so beautiful and fragile that they should just be left to grow!

HAWKBIT: AUTUMN

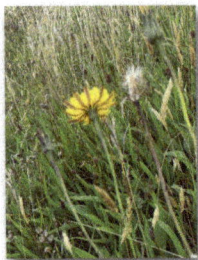

LATIN NAME: Leontodon autumnalis

COMMON NAME: Fall Dandelion; no other names found

BEST TIME TO SEE: June - October

FLOWER COLOUR: Yellow with brown sepals behind flowers

HEIGHT/STEM LENGTH: up to 60cm

🌼 Autumn Hawkbit is so like the Spring Catsear, that the only way to tell the difference seems to be to look at the calendar! The genus name for the Autumn Hawkbit is Leontodon, the Latin word for Lion's Tooth, and refers to the jagged ends of the flower petals.

🌼 The plants produce floods of yellow blooms on the mown slopes and in hedgerows, particularly after harvest.

🌼 The plant is an indicator of ancient meadows, so it is a bonus when you see it flowering. It provides food for larvae and adults of day-flying moths and bumblebees, and is a food source for birds.

A FASCINATING FACT

The Hawkbit name may have come from an ancient belief that hawks ate the plant to improve their eyesight. However there is no proof that it works!

HAWKWEED: ORANGE

LATIN NAME: Pilosella aurantiaca

COMMON NAMES: Fox & Cubs;
Devil's Paintbrush; Grim the Collier

BEST TIME TO SEE: June - October

FLOWER COLOUR: Orange; Centre
yellow

HEIGHT/STEM LENGTH: up to 40cm

🌾 Commonly known as Fox and Cubs, this plant is known for its one large orange flower (the fox), which is surrounded by smaller buds with orange 'noses' (the cubs).

🌾 The plant spreads by wind-blown, floating, dandelion-like seeds as well as by runners along the ground, and can create large colonies, invading fields and hedgerows.

🌾 In some areas, the plant is called Grim the Collier, referring to the black hairs on the plant's stems, leaves and sepals. The Latin name Pilosella means 'hairy'. Butterflies and pollinating flies love this plant, although the orange flowers are apparently invisible to some insects.

A FASCINATING FACT

Fox-and-Cubs produces a chemical that deters other plants from growing near it.

HAWTHORN

LATIN NAME: Crataegus monogyna

COMMON NAMES: May; Maytree; Thorn; Thornapple

BEST TIME TO SEE: May - June

FLOWER COLOUR: White or pale pink; Centres - yellow and pink

HEIGHT/STEM LENGTH: up to 10m

🌸 The flowers and buds of this shrub, often growing into a small, rounded tree, are classic blooms. Their round, white buds, white petals with pink stamens and yellow centres herald the Spring and have led to one of its most familiar names of May Blossom. May Queens would wear the flowers in their May Day celebrations.

🌸 Although used in May Day celebrations, in many districts people thought that May Blossom would bring Plague to any house where it was brought indoors. Recent research revealed that the flowers exude a chemical that also appears in decaying animals - no-one wants that smell in their house, so the legend must be true!

A FASCINATING FACT

Mice, bugs and slow worms love the shiny red haws, sheltering among the thorny thickets at the foot of the bushes where they are safe from predators.

HEATHER

LATIN NAME: Calluna vulgaris

COMMON NAMES: Common Heather; Ling

BEST TIME TO SEE: August - September

FLOWER COLOUR: Bells - from dark pink to purple

HEIGHT/STEM LENGTH: up to 60cm

🌿 Ling is the most common heather species in the UK. The green shoots are one of the first signs of upland Spring and the purple flowers coat the hills and moorlands in late Summer.

🌿 In fields near moorlands, these plants constantly try to invade field margins, hedgerows, paths and walls with their strong roots and wiry stems.

🌿 The name derives from either the old Norse 'lyng' or from the Anglo-Saxon 'lig', meaning a fire, and Heather is still a fuel in some remote areas.

🌿 At one time, a Heather mattress was thought to be more comfortable than a feather bed.

A FASCINATING FACT

Heather flowers are believed to bring luck, particularly if you find a plant with white flowers, because pink or red flowers are thought to have been stained by blood.

HERB BENNET

LATIN NAME: Geum urbanum

COMMON NAMES: Wood Avens;
Colewort; Saint Benedict's Herb

BEST TIME TO SEE: May - August

FLOWER COLOUR: Tepals - yellow;
Centre - yellow

HEIGHT/STEM LENGTH: up to 70cm

- Herb Bennet is another unobtrusive flower that blooms in shade and always looks slightly sad, as its yellow petals are often misshapen or even missing, showing its buds and sepals as it flowers among its hairy leaves.

- Herb Bennet seed heads are brown spiky burrs with tiny hooks that catch in animal fur or human clothing, often becoming very difficult to remove.

- Herb Bennet roots, which taste of cloves, have been used as a natural flavouring for beer, wine and liqueurs. They are used as a substitute for cloves, as they smell and taste similar, and the flavour improves as the herb is dried.

A FASCINATING FACT

The young leaves of Herb Bennet, when deep fried, apparently puff up like prawn crackers or crispy Chinese seaweed, to make a tasty snack, but I have never tried it.

HERB ROBERT

LATIN NAME: Geranium Robertianum

COMMON NAMES: Red Robin; Death Come Quickly; Storksbill; Squinter-pip

BEST TIME TO SEE: May - August

FLOWER COLOUR: White or pale pink; Centre - bright pink

HEIGHT/STEM LENGTH: 10 - 40cm

- All plants named Robin or Robert have a traditional link with devils, death and the fairy folk. Herb Robert, with its little pink flowers and red-tinged foliage, grows in hedges, walls and yards, and is another in the group of small and tenacious wild plants. When squashed, its leaves will emit an unpleasant, mousy scent.

- The flowers ripen into the stork's bill-shaped seed heads, typical of the geranium family, and giving the plant one of its common names.

- An insect repellant made from the plant can be rubbed on the skin and is said to be very effective against mosquitoes. It is also said to deter fleas in pet bedding.

A FASCINATING FACT

The rubbery smell of the sap of Herb Robert makes it a good companion plant for the vegetable or fruit garden, as it repels insect pests.

HOGWEED

LATIN NAME: Heracleum sphondylium

COMMON NAMES: Cow Parsnip; Eltrot

BEST TIME TO SEE: May - September

FLOWER COLOUR: White/pink; Central stamens long and white

HEIGHT/STEM LENGTH: Up to 180cm

🌿 Both the roots and the flower buds of this rather hairy plant with starry white flowers can be eaten. One of the interesting features of the plant, with its 'piggy' name, is the way the flower buds grow in a papery covering like a ready-made parcel, which can be left on if you steam the buds to eat as a vegetable.

🌿 Insects, particularly ladybirds, hoverflies, beetles and little field flies love this plant, gathering on the flat flower heads in Summer, feeding and breeding on the complex, creamy-white flower heads.

🌿 True to its name, pigs love this plant and will dig deep in the ground for the roots.

A FASCINATING FACT

Traditionally, the hollow stems of this plant were used in children's games - for water guns, pea-shooters or swords.

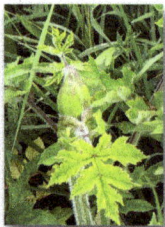

Why not try some of these old games on your walks?

HONESTY

LATIN NAME: Lunaria annua

COMMON NAMES: Moonwort; Money Plant; Silver Dollars

BEST TIME TO SEE: March - May

FLOWER COLOUR: Bright pink or purple; seeds silvery white

HEIGHT/STEM LENGTH: 20 - 100cm

🌿 Honesty flowers bloom in bright magenta spires above their purple tinged foliage. They like damp, shady hedgerows and ditches. The beautiful fragrant flowers are also attractive to pollinating insects.

🌿 The Latin name Lunaria means 'moon-shaped' and refers to the shape and appearance of the seedpods, which develop on the plants in late summer and hang there like brown purses, eventually losing their external coverings to reveal silvery white pennies.

🌿 If you find Honesty flowers, don't expect to see them again the next year. They are biennials, taking two years to grow, but the flowers will come, followed by the silver seeds, which you can gather for your home.

A FASCINATING FACT

All parts of the plant, particularly the seeds, are poisonous <u>to cats</u> but not to humans. However, typical of cats, most show little interest in it!

HORSETAIL: FIELD

LATIN NAME: Equisetum arvense

COMMON NAMES: Mare's Tail;
Snake Grass; Pipeweed; Puzzle Grass

TIME TO SEE: August - September

FLOWER COLOUR: Flowers tiny,
brown/green, almost invisible

HEIGHT/STEM LENGTH:: up to 80cm

🌿 The strange shoots of Field Horsetail have clear sections, with a fruiting body at the top. The plant is easily recognised in Spring and Summer by its upright, light green, asparagus-like shoots with folded needle-like leaves drooping outward in frilly rings around the stem. It likes dappled shade or sun, and damp round its roots. It can also be found growing in Spring woodlands.

🌿 Horsetail is one of the oldest plants in the world, having survived for over 100 million years. Some plants were trees up to 30m. tall.

🌿 One fruiting cone from one plant can produce 100,000 spores, spreading to colonise nearby areas, becoming established and hard to remove.

A FASCINATING FACT

It is said that the pattern of nodes in horsetail stems - which are increasingly close together, inspired John Napier to discover mathematical logarithms.

KNAPWEED

LATIN NAME: Centaurea nigra

COMMON NAMES: Hardheads; Iron Knobs; Centaury; Basket Flower

TIME TO SEE: June - September

FLOWER COLOUR: Magenta pink or purple

HEIGHT/STEM LENGTH: 20 to 80cm

🌸 Descriptive names for the purple flowers of Knapweed are 'Hardheads', or 'Basket Flower', describing the hard, brown, basket-patterned seed vessels below the purple flowers.

🌸 Knapweed is one of our toughest meadow plants. It is in bloom from June to September, and is a firm favourite of a wide range of pollinating insects, as a source of high quality nectar. In surveys it has been rated in the top five flowers for nectar production.

🌸 The herbalist Culpeper advises 'For the bite of a viper (the adder) drink Knapweed and water.'

A FASCINATING FACT

The Latin name refers to Chiron the centaur, who was said to have used the herb to heal his hoof when it was injured.

LADY'S MANTLE

LATIN NAME: Alchemilla mollis

COMMON NAMES: Stellaria; Hairless Lady's Mantle; Lion's Foot

BEST TIME TO SEE: May - September

FLOWER COLOUR: Sepals - greeny yellow; Centre - greeny yellow

HEIGHT/STEM LENGTH: up to 60cm

🌿 The yellowy-green flowers of Lady's Mantle are tiny; but the mantle or cloak-shaped leaves are flamboyantly frilly and softly hairy. The leaves give the plant its name and its fame, as they capture rain and dew, holding drops like jewels, shining in the sun.

🌿 Alchemists once thought that the shining drops had magical powers, and that they could use these to transform base metals into gold. They collected them carefully, but there is no evidence that they had any success.

🌿 Lady's Mantle is very invasive and is difficult to remove. It has spread to the wild from gardens.

A FASCINATING FACT

Pick the flowers before they set seed, and dry them to decorate your home.

Lady's Mantle will also. produce a pale yellow natural dye.

LADY'S SMOCK

LATIN NAME: Cardamine pratensis
COMMON NAMES: Cuckoo Flower; Fairy Flower
BEST TIME TO SEE: May - June
FLOWER COLOUR: Pale pink; Centre - white/yellow
HEIGHT/STEM LENGTH: 15 - 60cm

❦ Lady's Smock flowers, in clusters of palest pink wave gently on their thin stalks as Spring moves towards summer, and the grasses begin to get taller. The plant loves damp places and will often colonise boggy areas, and meadows where water flows underground.

❦ The flowers appear around the time when the call of the cuckoo is first heard in country areas, and gives the plant one of its most familiar names of Cuckoo Flower. The four petals of the delicate flowers are streaked with darker pink to lead insects to the flower's centre.

A FASCINATING FACT

One of this flower's country names is Thunder Flower, as picking Lady's Smock flowers was believed to immediately bring a thunderstorm down on your head!

LETTUCE: WALL

LATIN NAME: Mycelis muralis

COMMON NAMES: Hedge Lettuce; Wildflower Lettuce; Dock-cress; ivy-leaved lettuce

BEST TIME TO SEE: July - September

FLOWER COLOUR: Lemon yellow; Centre - yellow

HEIGHT/STEM LENGTH: 25 - 100cm

🌿 Wall lettuce is a fairy-thin, spindly plant that can easily be overlooked. It rewards a closer look, with its little yellow, orange-tinged flowers on reddish stems, making a network of light against a shady wall, fence or ditch bank, where the flowers shine like little stars.

🌿 The seeds are in bright black seed capsules, which have airy parachutes, and fairy-like they float off gently on the wind to establish new colonies, sometimes several fields away from the original parent plant. They may be considered by some people to be a nuisance, but they are so delicate and lovely that I hope they don't get eradicated!

A FASCINATING FACT

Wall Lettuce can produce 500 seeds on each plant, and a large plant can produce up to 11,000 seeds! The seeds can stay viable in the ground for 2 years.

LUNGWORT

LATIN NAME: Pulmonaria officinalis

COMMON NAMES: Joseph and Mary, Soldiers and Sailors

BEST TIME TO SEE: February - May

FLOWER COLOUR: Pink/blue/purple

HEIGHT/STEM LENGTH: 25cm

◈ Lungwort, or pulmonaria is another escape from gardens, now naturalised in many wild areas.

◈ The flowers are fascinating. They vary in colour from purple, violet or blue to shades of pink and red, and sometimes white. The colour of the flower in bud is often pink to violet when they first emerge, which then changes to blue as the flowers mature. The plant is covered in hairs of varied length and stiffness, and the leaves are often covered in white spots.

◈ People take lungwort to treat breathing conditions, stomach and intestinal ailments, and kidney and urinary tract problems. Lungwort is also used in cough medicines, to relieve fluid retention, and to treat lung diseases such as tuberculosis.

A FASCINATING FACT

The name Lungwort derives from the leaves resembling ulcerated lung tissue.

MARIGOLD: CORN

LATIN NAME: Glebionis segetum

SOME COMMON NAMES: Corn Daisy; Yellow Daisy; Boodle; Bozzom; Buddle

BEST TIME TO SEE: June - October

FLOWER COLOUR: Outer ray florets - bright yellow; Centre - yellow

HEIGHT/STEM LENGTH: 20 - 60cm

🌿 The bright yellow daisy-like flowers of the Corn Marigold sometimes appear where excavations have disturbed ancient land, exposing seeds which have lain dormant, often for many years. So if you see them, they are unlikely to reappear in following years, as the flowers may be sterile.

🌿 Corn Marigolds have declined until they are now a rarity and are only common where wild flower seed has been planted, often mixed with old plants such as Corncockle and Corn Poppy in attempts to re-colonise ancient meadowland. This is where most of us are likely to see them, where they may be confused with garden varieties of Marigold.

A FASCINATING FACT

Like all plants of the Chrysanthemum family, Corn Marigolds are loved by Honey bees, Carder Bees and Hoverflies.

MAYWEED: SCENTED

LATIN NAME: Matricaria recutita

COMMON NAMES: Wild Chamomile; Dog Fennel; Stinking Mayweed

BEST TIME TO SEE: May - June

FLOWER COLOUR: Outer ray florets - white; Centre - bright yellow

HEIGHT/STEM LENGTH: 10 - 50cm

🌿 The Mayweed plant has white flowers, backward facing petals with conical yellow centres, and thin leaves. It has a scrambling habit, producing long, floppy stems which lean on other plants. It grows in arable fields and hay meadows. The whole plant has a pungent smell.

🌿 Scented Mayweed is a very ancient plant, and garlands of the flowers were found decorating the body of the King Tutankhamen in his tomb.

🌿 Ladybirds and other insects love the flowers, but bees do not visit - maybe they don't like the smell!

A FASCINATING FACT

Deep blue and yellow oils can be distilled from the flowers.

A NOTE ON TOXICITY

Mayweed juice can blister the skin, and upset the stomach.

MEDICK: BLACK

LATIN NAME: Medicago lupulina

COMMON NAMES: Nonesuch; Hop Clover; Hop Medic; Black Hay

BEST TIME TO SEE: April - August

FLOWER COLOUR: Yellow; Centre - not visible

HEIGHT/STEM LENGTH: 5 - 25cm

Like all true clovers, Black Medick has groups of three little leaves joined together, and small yellow flower heads. Their little clover-like flowers reward a second look, as they create a bright yellow foil to the blooms of Buttercups, Bluebells, Mouse-ear and Red Clover.

The second part of its Latin name, 'lupulina', means wolf-like, but this links it to the Hop plant and not with wolves!

Black Medick is also a crucial source of nectar and pollen for honey bees as it produces flowers over a long flowering season.

A FASCINATING FACT

A 'pioneer plant', Medick is often one of the first to appear when land has been disturbed. Its roots host nitrogen-fixing bacteria, bringing nutrients to other plants in the same area.

MIGNONETTE

LATIN NAME: Reseda lutea

COMMON NAMES: Weld; Dyer's Rocket; Bastard Rocket

BEST TIME TO SEE: June - September

FLOWER COLOUR: Yellow

HEIGHT/STEM LENGTH: 50cm

- In high summer the pale greenish yellow spires of the wild mignonette stand out amongst the grassland in which they are generally found. It grows best on well-drained soils in open habitats, occurring on waste ground and roadside verges, in marginal grassland, disused railway land, quarries and arable land, in disturbed chalk and limestone grassland.

- The leaves are eaten by the caterpillars of various butterflies, including the Cabbage White, Bath White and Orange Tip.

- Mignonette is used in flower arrangements and potpourri. The volatile oil is used in perfumes, and was also used as a sedative and a treatment for bruises. The leaves and flowers have been used to make a yellow dye called 'weld'.

A FASCINATING FACT

The name 'mignonette' comes from the French 'mignon', meaning 'dainty', and in the Language of Flowers mignonette means 'Your qualities surpass your charms'.

MOUSE-EAR

LATIN NAME: Cerastium fontanum

SOME COMMON NAMES: Mouse-ear Chickweed; Star Chickweed; Starweed

BEST TIME TO SEE: April - September

FLOWER COLOUR: White; Centre - creamy white

HEIGHT/STEM LENGTH: up to 50cm

🌿 Mouse-ear is a member of the huge Chickweed family. It grows all over hay meadows, among the grasses and flowers, and has a sprawling habit, with long tendrils of leaves and white flowers. Each flower has petals like pairs of little mouse ears lifting their heads above surrounding grasses. Low growing, it can recover very quickly after mowing.

🌿 Each plant can produce up to 6,500 seeds, surviving in the soil for as long as 40 years, even without a parent plant nearby. Seeds can also germinate after being eaten by cows or birds.

A FASCINATING FACT

All Chickweeds have this interesting habit in common - they spend every night with their leaves folded over to protect the young buds and new shoots, opening them again the next morning.

NETTLE: COMMON

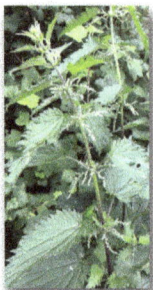

LATIN NAME: Urtica dioica

SOME COMMON NAMES: Stinging
Nettle; Bigsting Nettle; Slendernettle

BEST TIME TO SEE: June - October

FLOWER COLOUR: Long tassels of tiny
greenish yellow flowers with green
stamens

HEIGHT/STEM LENGTH: up to 150cm

🌿 The green Stinging Nettle is a familiar hazard
to anyone who walks in country fields and
woods, particularly with adventurous children.
Nettles grow in the edges of fields and on any
rough ground, preferably in damp soil. The
plants often develop into large colonies,
spreading by roots on or near the surface.

🌿 The flowers are insignificant green tassels, but
very popular with butterflies and ladybirds that
lay their eggs underneath the leaves. The larvae
and caterpillars then munch through the leaves
apparently totally immune to
the stings.

🌿 If you want to attract insects
to your garden, grow a nettle
patch in a corner!

A FASCINATING FACT

Nettles have been used for years
to make a soft fabric for shirts
and jackets, and uniforms for soldiers. You can
still buy shirts made from nettles.

ORCHID: COMMON SPOTTED

LATIN NAME: Dactilorhyza fuchsii

COMMON NAMES: Common Spotted Orchid

BEST TIME TO SEE: June - July

FLOWER COLOUR: White with pale pink, and darker pink markings

HEIGHT/STEM LENGTH: 10 - 15cm

🌷 Of the 50 different wild orchid species flourishing in the UK, the Common Spotted Orchid is one of the few Orchid species that you may see among the Spring grasses in natural hay meadows. They have spires of pale pink flowers, spotted with darker pink on the lips of each floret. However, they will sometimes appear in one year, then mysteriously disappear for years or even for ever.

🌷 The pods of the Vanilla orchid are still used in many Middle Eastern countries to flavour all sorts of foods, but although Orchid petals are sometimes used as a garnish, they are not eaten in the UK.

A FASCINATING FACT

Some people once thought orchids were poisonous for cats, dogs and horses, but this has recently been disproved.

PIGNUT

LATIN NAME: Conopodium majus

SOME COMMON NAMES: Kippernut; Earth Chestnut; St Anthony's Nut

BEST TIME TO SEE: March-October

FLOWER COLOUR: White; Centre stamens long and white

HEIGHT/STEM LENGTH: 8 - 50cm

〰 Pignut is a small, dainty member of the Carrot or Parsley family, which flowers in lacy white across hay meadows and verges from early Spring, returning to flower again after the harvest, and well into the early months of winter. Its little florets, on thin stalks, can stand high winds and rainstorms, shrugging off all sorts of weather.

〰 Pignut is a sign that the land has been left undisturbed for many years, and is one indicator of very ancient pasture.

〰 Even though Pignut is edible, perhaps we should leave this harmless little plant to grow, and refrain from eating it.

A FASCINATING FACT

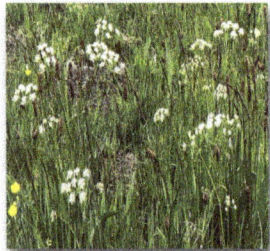

Pigs love the roots of Pignut, and so do human foragers, who have said that they taste of Chestnut, Hazelnut, or Brazil Nut.

PINK PURSLANE

LATIN NAME: Claytonia sibirica

COMMON NAMES: Candy Flower; Chinese Chickweed; Indian Lettuce; Miner's Lettuce; Spring Beauty

BEST TIME TO SEE: April - July

FLOWER COLOUR: Pink

HEIGHT/STEM LENGTH: 40cm

🌸 A succulent, tasty plant, with an almost beetroot like earthy flavour, that can be found throughout the year, it has pink flowers from April to July.

🌸 The whole plant is edible but the spoon shaped basal leaves are the sweetest especially in Winter or Spring.

🌸 Purslane can play a role in improving vision and healthy mucus membranes and to protect from some cancers. A poultice of the chewed leaves can be applied to cuts and sores, and the juice of the plant has been used as eye drops for sore red eyes, and a cold infusion of the stems has been used as an antidandruff shampoo.

A FASCINATING FACT

Purslane is rich in vitamin A which is a natural antioxidant. The plant is one of the highest in vitamin A of all green leafy vegetables.

PLANTAIN: RIBWORT

LATIN NAME: Plantago lanceolata

COMMON NAMES: Ribgrass; Wagbread; Rippleseed

BEST TIME TO SEE: March - August

FLOWER COLOUR: Brown and very tiny; Anthers - long and white

HEIGHT/STEM LENGTH: 10 - 50cm

🌿 Ribwort Plantain, with its dark, greeny-brown buds, explodes into fireworks of little white petals. It is a common, often overlooked plant in most meadows. It is one of the first plants to appear. It is certainly one of the first to flower, sparkling across the spring fields, and it continues to flower throughout the Spring and early Summer, starring the meadows among the other Spring flowers and grasses.

🌿 The leaves and seeds of Ribwort Plantain provide nutritious food for grazing stock, and farmers thought of it as a grass, calling it 'Ribgrass'.

🌿 Plantain seed heads provide winter food for Goldfinches and many other seed-eating birds that forage in the fields.

A FASCINATING FACT

The roots are said to be a cure for snake bites.

POPPY: WELSH

LATIN NAME: Meconopsis cambrica

COMMON NAMES: Welsh Poppy; Papaver Cambricum

BEST TIME TO SEE: May - August

FLOWER COLOUR: Bright yellow or orange; Centre - yellow with a green middle

HEIGHT/STEM LENGTH: 30 - 60cm

- The bright orange and yellow flowers of the Welsh Poppy, with their thin petals, crumpled from the bud, lean out from walls and between rocks, opening their petals to relax in the sun.

- Poppies attract a wide variety of insects, including bees and hoverflies, seeking pollen from the wide open flowers. Seed numbers per plant can range from 10,000 to 60,000, and this has helped the plant to escape to the wild, where it is now impossible to eradicate.

- These poppies seem to be as at home here as in Wales, where the flower has been adopted as a logo by Plaid Cymru.

A FASCINATING FACT

The Welsh Poppy is not a true poppy. It doesn't have the 'pepperpot' seed head of a true poppy, but sheds its seeds through slits in the seed head.

RAGWORT

LATIN NAME: Senecio jacobaea
COMMON NAMES: Stinking Willie;
Benweed; St. James-Wort; Stammerwort
BEST TIME TO SEE: June - November
FLOWER COLOUR: Outer rays - yellow;
Inner florets yellow
HEIGHT/STEM LENGTH: 30 - 150cm

- Ragwort, with its pretty yellow flowers appears in fields just before harvest, and, as it is poisonous to animals even after drying, farmers will try to remove it all before mowing.

- The flowers lift their sunny heads in the middle of fields and in the field margins, and the flat-topped flowers attract over 70 different species of insects, including flies, bees, wasps, butterflies, moths, as well as the stripey caterpillars of the Cinnabar Moth.

- One plant can produce 2,000 to 2,500 yellow flowers in a single season, and as many as 75,000 to 120,000 seeds spread by the wind, making it very difficult to control.

A FASCINATING FACT

The leaves will produce a green dye, and the flowers produce yellow, brown or orange natural dyes. These will both work best on natural fibres such as cotton or linen.

136

RASPBERRY

LATIN NAME: Rubus idaeus

COMMON NAMES: Hindberry;
Brambleberry; Raspis; Wild Red

BEST TIME TO SEE: June - September

FLOWER COLOUR: Pink or white; Central
parts - pale yellow; Fruit - deep pinkish red

HEIGHT/STEM LENGTH: up to 1.5m

🌺 Wild Raspberries grow and produce their pale flowers and ruby red fruit in many hedgerows across the UK. They probably escaped some years ago from country gardens or grew from seeds dropped by birds or small animals. The bushes are a welcome sight to passers-by as they hang their red fruits among rough leaves and chalky, prickly canes.

🌺 Raspberries have a two year growth cycle. In the first year the plant grows one cane with just leaves, but in the second year this cane produces branches with leaves, flowers and fruit.

🌺 Tempting and tasty as they are, it is perhaps kinder to leave the berries on the canes for field mice and other small mammals to enjoy.

A FASCINATING FACT

The berries are popular with birds and insects as well, as they contain more vitamin C than oranges. The raspberry is a symbol for kindness.

138

ROSE: WILD

LATIN NAME: Rosa canina

COMMON NAMES: Dog Rose; Bird Briar; Dog Berry; Witches' Briar

BEST TIME TO SEE: June – July

FLOWER COLOUR: Pink/pale pink; Centre - dark yellow with yellow

HEIGHT/STEM LENGTH: up to 3m

- The pale pink, gently scented Wild Rose, or Dog Rose is one of the most beautiful country flowers, winding its woody branches through hedges, holding up its delicate pink flowers, each with a ring of yellow stamens to tempt pollinators.

- The name Dog Rose was used at a time when people thought the root was a cure for the bite of a mad dog.

- The flowers are followed by eye catching red rose-hips which stay on the prickly stems until the winter, as welcome food for birds, mice, voles and other small mammals.

A FASCINATING FACT

During the Second World War, country children were paid to collect rose hips to make the Vitamin C rich, pink Rose-hip Syrup, used to compensate for the poor wartime diet.

ST JOHN'S WORT: COMMON

LATIN NAME: Hypericum calycinum

COMMON NAMES: Tipton Weed; Aaron's Beard; Rose of Sharon

BEST TIME TO SEE: June - September

FLOWER COLOUR: Yellow; Stamens - very long and yellow

HEIGHT/STEM LENGTH: up to 60 cm

🌿 The showy, golden firework flowers of this plant, with long, silky stamens surrounded by bright yellow petals, betray its origins as a popular garden flower before escaping to the countryside. It now flowers in hedges and waste ground. The common name refers to its traditional flowering and harvesting on St John's Day, 24th of June, when red spots are reputed to appear on the leaves.

🌿 The flowers and leaves of the plant are used in teas and as a dietary supplement to treat mental health problems, stress and other conditions.

A NOTE ON TOXICITY

The flowers and berries are safe in herbal medicine, but fresh berries should not be eaten. Consult a doctor before starting a herbal course of St John's Wort. Find more information at:

nhs.uk/news/mental-health/st-johns-wort-for-depression

142

ST JOHN'S WORT: BUSHY

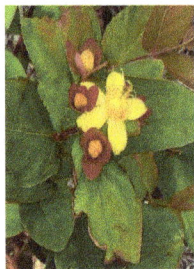

LATIN NAME: Hypericum androsaemum

COMMON NAMES: Tutsan; Lord God's Wonder Plant; Amber

BEST TIME TO SEE: June - September

FLOWER COLOUR: Yellow; Stamens - very long and yellow

HEIGHT/STEM LENGTH: 40 - 100cm

🌿 Tutsan, or Shrubby St John's Wort, is easy to confuse with the Common St John's Wort. Like all St John's Worts, this variety has yellow flowers with long stamens in the centres, but Tutsan also has very obvious red berries among the flowers, and these turn to shiny black as they ripen.

🌿 Tutsan is an extremely vigorous plant that spreads rapidly, and has a history of becoming a real nuisance, in spite of its value as a medicinal treatment to treat anxiety, depression and sleep problems.

A NOTE ON TOXICITY

The flowers and berries are safe in herbal medicine, but fresh berries should not be eaten. Consult a doctor before starting a herbal course of St John's Wort. Find more information at:

nhs.uk/news/mental-health/st-johns-wort-for-depression

SALAD BURNET

LATIN NAME: Sanguisorba minor

SOME COMMON NAMES: Drumsticks, Old Man's Pepper and Poor Man's Pepper

BEST TIME TO SEE: May - August

FLOWER COLOUR: Green; Stamens Red/Yellow

HEIGHT/STEM LENGTH: 30cm

🌺 The flowers of Salad Burnet are in a round flowerhead up to 2cm across. Square stems bear small deeply-toothed leaves, either in opposite pairs or alternate, ending with a trefoil leaf.

🌺 The flowers are small, and in a globular or ovoid head, with the most prominent feature being the numerous short red styles protruding from each flower, like miniature shaving brushes. Individual flowers have 4 green sepals (no petals), often tinged purple and become more purple when older. The lower flowers in the head contain multiple, dangly, yellow stamens.

🌺 The leaves and flowers are edible, and Salad Burnet also has medicinal uses. It has been used to control bleeding and was also used against the Plague. Brewed into a tea, it has been used to relieve diarrhoea..

A FASCINATING FACT

The whole plant smells of cucumber!

SCABIOUS: DEVIL'S BIT

LATIN NAME: Succisa pratensis

COMMON NAMES: Bobby Bright Buttons

BEST TIME TO SEE: July - October

FLOWER COLOUR: Blue/mauve

HEIGHT/STEM LENGTH: Up to 75cm

🌿 The Devil's Bit Scabious is a less common form of scabious, but grows alongside it. This variety has tight domes of tiny flowers with little stigmas sticking out. Opening from July until October, they provide a valuable late source of nectar and pollen and are loved by bees and butterflies.

🌿 Devil's Bit Scabious is also a vital food plant for the declining Marsh Fritillary Butterfly.

🌿 In folk tales the short black root was bitten off by the devil, angry at the plant's ability to cure skin ailments such as scabies.

🌿 The Devil's Bit Scabious gets its Latin name from 'Scabere', meaning to scratch - it has been traditionally used as a treatment for skin conditions, such as scabies and the sores of bubonic plague.

A FASCINATING FACT

This scabious is a member of the teasel family of plants.

SCABIOUS: MEADOW

LATIN NAME: Knautia arvensis

COMMON NAMES: Pins-and-Needles; Snake Flower; Curl-Doddy (Curly Head); Lady's Pincushion; Bachelor's Buttons; Blue Bonnets.

BEST TIME TO SEE: July - September

FLOWER COLOUR: Blue/pink/white

HEIGHT/STEM LENGTH: 1m

- The flower head of the Scabious is composed of many small individual flowers, each of which has four unequal petals. The stems and leaves are rough and hairy, similar in texture to scabby skin.

- Scabious seem to attract every pollinating insect. The flower has a very long flowering period, so it is a valuable nectar source for bees and butterflies. Each plant can produce up to 50 flowers and blooms are the largest of our native scabious species. Finches and Linnets particularly love the seeds of this plant.

- The juice of 'scabiosa herba' was given to alleviate plague sores, eczema, rashes and cracked skin.

A FASCINATING FACT

In Belgium girls would pick Scabious buds, give each a lover's name, and then choose a husband by the one that produced the best flowers.

SELF-HEAL

LATIN NAME: Prunella vulgaris

COMMON NAMES: Brunella; Heart-of-the-Earth; Carpenter's Herb; Blue Curls

BEST TIME TO SEE: June - October

FLOWER COLOUR: Purple

HEIGHT/STEM LENGTH: up to 20cm

🌿 Self-heal's bright purple, boxy flower heads and purple tinted leaves make a strong statement in the dips of fields or in the shade of walls and hedges, sometimes flowering in big colonies under hedges or in ditches. It blooms from early Spring to Autumn, later at higher altitudes.

🌿 In common with others in the Dead Nettle family, Self-heal is particularly attractive to bees. It flowers in June, ready to provide yet another nectar source for bees and wasps, continuing to bloom well into Autumn, after the harvest has removed other food sources.

A FASCINATING FACT

Self-heal is a member of the Mint family, but many who try it think it tastes more of Rosemary, and the plant does contain rosmaric acid.

SHEEP'S SORREL

LATIN NAME: Rumex acetosella

COMMON NAMES: Red Sorrel; Sour Weed; Field Sorrel

BEST TIME TO SEE: March - October

FLOWER COLOUR: Petals - none; Sepals - green and red

HEIGHT/STEM LENGTH: 5 - 30cm

- This small, dainty member of the Dock family, Sheep's Sorrel grows with slender, reddish stems, leaves and seed heads which decorate hay meadows before the hay is harvested, when the sunlit fields glow red with their spires in the evening sunset.

- Sheep's Sorrel is a valuable core plant of upland hay meadows, adding to diversity and providing a long season of seeds for all sorts of animals and birds.

- Sheep's sorrel seeds are a staple food of many small meadow birds, particularly the little endangered bird called the Twite, which nests in the heather of northern moorlands, and feeds Sorrel seeds to its young.

A FASCINATING FACT

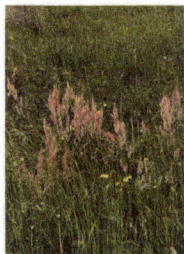

The leaves of Sheep's Sorrel have a flavour like apple peel or citrus lemon, and can be used to sweeten cakes and sorbets.

SNOWDROP

LATIN NAME: Galanthus nivalis

COMMON NAMES: Candlemas Bells; Mary's Taper; Snow Piercer; February Fairmaids; Dingle-Dangle

BEST TIME TO SEE: January - March

FLOWER COLOUR: White

HEIGHT/STEM LENGTH: Up to 25cm

🌿 Snowdrops have no petals, and are composed of six white flower segments known as tepals which look like petals. The inner three tepals are smaller and have a notch in the tip, with a green upturned 'v'.

🌿 Despite a long history in the UK, where the Snowdrop is a favourite sign of Spring, it may not be native here. It was not recorded as growing wild in the UK until the late 18th century, when it escaped from gardens, making the white snowdrop 'valleys' we can now see.

🌿 Snowdrops do not need pollinating insects, instead, they spread via bulb division. However, they may still be visited by bees and other insects on a warm Spring day.

A FASCINATING FACT

In Yorkshire, on February 2nd, the feast of the Virgin Mary, village girls gathered bunches of Snowdrops and wore them as a symbol of purity.

SOW THISTLE

LATIN NAME: Sonchus asper

COMMON NAMES: Hare's Lettuce;
Hare's Colwort; Hare's Thistle

BEST TIME TO SEE: July - September

FLOWER COLOUR: Yellow

HEIGHT/STEM LENGTH: 20 - 75cm

- This plant is tall, thin and straggly, with little yellow, dandelion-like flowers, and prefers to grow where it has some protection from the wind for its long stalks and nodding flower heads.

- The name Sow-thistle comes from its habit of exuding a latex like milk which was believed to help lactation, particularly in mothering sows.

- The feathery Sow-thistle seeds are wind dispersed and some seeds have been collected by aircraft at 2,000 ft. The seeds are loved by birds, but hated by farmers, as the plant is so invasive.

- This plant often grows around trees and fence posts and along path edges,   and is likely to have been visited by dogs, so take care if you collect the plant for food!

A FASCINATING FACT

The latex in the sap has been used in the treatment of warts. The Romans used Thistle latex as an early sort of chewing gum.

SPEEDWELL:FIELD

LATIN NAME: Veronica persica

COMMON NAMES: Birdeye Speedwell, Gypsyweed; Cat's Eye; Eye of the Child Jesus; Farewell; Goodbye

BEST TIME TO SEE: January - December

FLOWER COLOUR: Bright blue

HEIGHT/STEM LENGTH: 10-30cm

🌼 The bright eyes of Speedwell sparkle through hedges and grassland throughout the summer, reflecting the blue of a Summer day.

🌼 The Latin name 'Veronica' comes from a story of a woman, later canonised as St. Veronica who is said to have wiped the blood from the face of Jesus on his journey to Calvary. Afterwards, her kerchief was thought to bear the 'vera iconica', the true likeness, of his sacred features.' 'Vera iconica' is actually a mixture of Greek and Latin terms.

🌼 A tea made of speedwell is used to clear sinus congestion, help eyesight, and ease sore eyes.

🌼 Speedwell is thought to be a blood purifier, removing excess mucus, soothing internal tissues, coughs, asthma and pleurisy.

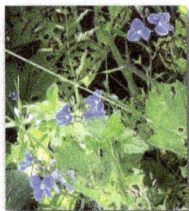

A FASCINATING FACT

Field Speedwell produces seeds but it can also spread vegetatively from bits of stem.

SPEEDWELL: HEATH

LATIN NAME: Veronica officinalis

COMMON NAMES: Drug Speedwell; Common Speedwell; Paul's Betony

BEST TIME TO SEE: May - August

FLOWER COLOUR: White, pale mauve or pink

HEIGHT/STEM LENGTH: up to 40cm

- Unlike its bright blue cousin the Germander Speedwell, this little flower produces delicate lilac blooms in little spires among the grasses in the field margins, but more commonly in woodlands, on heathland, and at the edges of paths.

- Speedwell was believed to improve mental health problems, and has been taken for many years as a calming tonic.

- A salve or ointment made from the dried and steeped leaves of Heath Speedwell can be applied to soothe bruises and other injuries.

A FASCINATING FACT

Saint Veronica gave Jesus a cloth to wipe his face on the way to Calvary. The marks on Speedwell flowers are said to resemble the marks left on her handkerchief. This gave the Veronica plant its name.

STITCHWORT

LATIN NAME: Stellaria holostea or Stellaria graminea (Lesser)

COMMON NAMES: Daddy's Shirt Buttons; Nanny Crackers; Poppers

BEST TIME TO SEE: March - June

FLOWER COLOUR: White; Centre -yellow

HEIGHT/STEM LENGTH: 15 - 80cm

🌿 Some of the smallest flowers are also some of the most delightful, and the little white flowers of Stitchwort shine out like stars from woodland edges and hedgerows in early Spring. Their thin stems scramble among stronger flowers, and some stems are nearly a metre long.

🌿 Stitchworts are common where Bluebells flower, and the white stars, which echo their name 'stellaria' or 'star-like', contrast with the colour of the blue bells. Lesser Stitchwort usually grows among the meadow grasses or in hedges.

🌿 Stitchworts are beneficial to many flying insects, including bees and butterflies (such as the Orange-Tip Butterfly).

A FASCINATING FACT

Earning names of Snapdragon or Nanny Crackers, the seed pods will explode with a loud 'pop' if you disturb them. The leaves were used to ease 'stitch' in the side.

STRAWBERRY: WILD

LATIN NAME: Fragaria vesca

SOME COMMON NAMES: Woodland or Alpine or European Strawberry

BEST TIME TO SEE: April - July

FLOWER COLOUR: White; with a yellow centre

HEIGHT/STEM LENGTH: 5 - 30cm

🌾 Small white flowers with starry yellow centres nestle among the green leaves on a sunny bank, giving clues to the presence of Wild Strawberries. The flowers and berries appear at the same time, but birds, wood mice, snails, slugs and other small creatures may get to the fruit before you!

🌾 Before cultivated strawberries were widely available and affordable, the wild strawberry was once a staple of country life, for jams, puddings and flavourings as well as for herbal treatments.

🌾 The berries are often small and sometimes mis-shapen, but their flavour is so good they are worth searching for. The fruit has traditionally been collected for cooking in gourmet restaurants, as the taste is so unique.

A FASCINATING FACT

Strawberry juice was used as a natural cure for chilblains, by washing your hands and feet in the juice.

THISTLE: CREEPING

LATIN NAME: Cirsium arvense

SOME COMMON NAMES: Lettuce of Hell; Cursed Thistle; Stinger Needles

BEST TIME TO SEE: July - October

FLOWER COLOUR: Pale pinkish purple; Centre - Pink/yellow

HEIGHT/STEM LENGTH: 20 - 120cm

- Creeping Thistle, with its pale lilac flowers and scaly buds with bright pink tips, is the UK's most widespread perennial Thistle.

- This thistle grows in big colonies in hay field margins, and favours old pastures and damp areas. Thistles are a real problem in hay meadows, so farmers are allowed to spot spray them, even in organic fields.

- Pollinators, specially butterflies love thistle flowers, but they are short lived as the flowers turn into fluffy seed heads within ten days. There can be between 1,600 to 50,000 seeds on a single plant, each one with a parachute, like a ghostly bone-coloured spider skeleton.

A FASCINATING FACT

Thistle down can be used as tinder to start camp or stove fires, and the roots were chewed as a treatment for toothache or indigestion.

THISTLE: MARSH

LATIN NAME: Cirsium palustre

COMMON NAMES: Marsh Plume
Thistle; European Swamp Thistle

BEST TIME TO SEE: July/September

FLOWER COLOUR: Dark magenta

HEIGHT: 30-200cm

- The first sign of a patch of these bright magenta flowers is often a flock of bright butterflies, bees and other insects, all attracted by the purple, nectar-filled flowers.

- The Marsh Thistle loves wet, neglected areas, where it often grows in big family groups, sometimes covered in butterflies, bees and other insects.

- In its first year it grows as a dense green rosette of leaves with spiny, dark purple edges. In following years each plant grows a tall, prickly stem, branching repeatedly, and bearing a wide candelabra of dark purple buds and flowers.

A FASCINATING FACT

Thistles yield a good oil, which is known as Safflower oil, an oil rich in Omega 3 and Omega 6 fatty acids.

THISTLE: MILK

LATIN NAME: Silybum marianum

SOME COMMON NAMES: Blessed Mary's Thistle; Blessed Thistle; Holy Thistle; Leaves of Mary

BEST TIME TO SEE: May - August

FLOWER COLOUR: Purple/red

HEIGHT/STEM LENGTH: 30-200cm

🌿 This prickly plant, a member of the sunflower family, has purple flowers, and the leaves have distinctive white veins, which tradition says were caused by a drop of the Virgin Mary's milk falling onto its leaves. The shiny black seeds, which are used medicinally, are collected at the end of summer when they are at their ripest and easiest to harvest.

🌿 Milk Thistle extract is made from the seeds, and these days research continues to support milk thistle's healing powers, especially for treating liver and blood problems as well as for intestinal cleaning, but results from studies have been inconclusive.

A FASCINATING FACT

In the Middle Ages the leaves and stalks of the milk thistle were used in salads, soups and pies, with the leaves said to surpass the finest cabbage. The heads were also eaten boiled and eaten like artichokes.

THISTLE: MUSK

LATIN NAME: Carduus nutans

SOME COMMON NAMES: Nodding Thistle, Nodding Plumeless Thistle

BEST TIME TO SEE: May - August

FLOWER COLOUR: Deep magenta pink

HEIGHT/STEM LENGTH: 1.5m

🌿 The Musk thistle has one large, nodding flower head on each stem comprised of bright pink florets (tiny flowers) fringed by spiny bracts. Its leaves are divided, with spiny lobes, and its stems are winged and cottony. The flower has a sweet, musky smell, hence the common name.

🌿 It is attractive to a wide range of insects, and is the food plant of the caterpillars of the Painted Lady Butterfly. Birds, such as Greenfinches and Linnets, also gorge on the seeds it produces.

🌿 The fleshy stem is edible and said to be delicious after peeling and boiling. Medicinally, the leaves have been used as a tonic to stimulate liver function, and the flowers have been used to reduce fever and purify the blood.

A FASCINATING FACT

A single flower head may produce 1,200 seeds and a single plant up to 120,000 seeds, which are wind dispersed. The seeds can remain viable in the soil for ten years, making it difficult to control.

174

TOADFLAX: IVY-LEAVED

LATIN NAME: Cymbalaria muralis

COMMON NAMES: Mother of Thousands; Oxford Ivy; Pennywort

BEST TIME TO SEE: April - October

FLOWER COLOUR: Purple; Centre - white and yellow

HEIGHT/STEM LENGTH: Up to 60cm

🌾 The little rounded, purple-tinged leaves of Ivy-leaved Toadflax often cover stone walls, clinging deep in the damp and dark cracks between stones and producing little purple snapdragon flowers with yellow mouths, irresistible to bees.

🌾 Toadflax is another non-native flower, imported into gardens and escaping to the wild. The common name 'Oxford Ivy' refers to one of the first places it was planted in walled gardens.

🌾 Ivy-leaved Toadflax has an unusual way of propagating. At first the flower stalk moves towards the light, but once the flower is fertilised, it turns away, pushing its seeds into the crevices of walls or into the ground to germinate. If you are very patient, you can watch this happening!

A FASCINATING FACT

The flowers and leaves are high in Vitamin C, and taste like watercress, but they should really be left for the bees!

TORMENTIL

LATIN NAME: Potentilla erecta

COMMON NAMES: Blood Root; Ewe Daisy; Biscuits; Shepherd's Knapperty

BEST TIME TO SEE: April - October

FLOWER COLOUR: Bright yellow

HEIGHT/STEM LENGTH: Up to 45cm

🌱 This bright yellow flower, with four heart-shaped petals, blooms in any warm place in a meadow or bank that faces South and gets direct sunshine. The number of petals make it easy to distinguish from Cinquefoils which have five petals.

🌱 The plant grows long tendrils that creep among the grasses, rooting before growing on, producing leaves and flowers as it covers large areas.

🌱 The Tormentil family all have a red dye in their roots, which gives them another name of Blood Root.

A FASCINATING FACT

Tormentil contains natural astringents, and is still widely used in cosmetics, shampoos, bath products, aftershave, skin creams, and deodorants.

TREFOIL: BIRD'S FOOT

LATIN NAME: Lotus corniculatus

COMMON NAMES: Eggs & Bacon; Granny's Toenails; lady's Slippers

TIME TO SEE: May - September

FLOWER COLOUR: Yellow, tinged with orange or red

HEIGHT/STEM LENGTH: 10 - 50cm

- Bird's Foot Trefoil is easily recognised by its bright yellow, red-tinted flowers, like tiny snapdragons, decorating a sunny bank or weaving through the grass in a meadow corner.

- The shape of the flowers and three-lobed leaves is typical of the pea family.

- The seed heads give the plant its name as they are shaped like a green bird's foot, with three toes, turning brown when ripe, and carrying seeds that ping open in warm sunshine. These seed pods must have given it one of the 70 different country names of 'Granny's Toenails'.

A NOTE ON TOXICITY

All parts of the <u>live</u> plant are poisonous. They can cause respiratory failure if eaten in quantity. The poisons disappear when the plant is dried, so animals can safely eat it mixed with hay.

VALERIAN

LATIN NAME: Centranthus ruber

SOME COMMON NAMES: Garden Heliotrope, All-Heal; Spur Valerian; Kiss-Me-Quick; Fox's Brush; Devil's Beard; Jupiter's Beard

BEST TIME TO SEE: May - October

FLOWER COLOUR: Red/pink/white

HEIGHT/STEM LENGTH: Up to 75cm

🌿 Valerian is native to the Mediterranean, imported as a garden plant, but soon escaped and became naturalised in the wild. Despite its non-native status, it is a good source of nectar from May to October for bees, butterflies and moths like the Hummingbird Hawk Moth.

🌿 Valerian is more closely related to the Teasel than to Wild Carrot, Hogweed or other umbellifers.

🌿 Medicine is made from the root. Valerian is most commonly used for sleep disorders, especially the inability to sleep (insomnia). Valerian is also used orally for anxiety and psychological stress, but there is limited scientific research to support these uses.

A FASCINATING FACT

The blooms have a strong and somewhat rank scent. Valerian is said to be very attractive to cats!

VETCH: BUSH

LATIN NAME: Vicia sepium

COMMON NAMES: None apart from Bush Vetch, no common names found

BEST TIME TO SEE: June - August

FLOWER COLOUR: Mauve and purple

HEIGHT/STEM LENGTH: 20 - 60cm

- Bush Vetch is one of many vetches growing in hay meadows, and one of three in meadows at higher altitudes. This little Vetch, with pea-like purple flowers, ladder-like, hairy leaves and stems, and deep black seed pods, grows freely in hay fields, scrambling among the tall grasses and other meadow flowers, with runners that can grow to 6m long, and roots up to 1m deep.

- Bush Vetch has nectaries at the base of its leaves which attract ants. These ants act as tiny bodyguards, keeping away the pests that like to munch the roots and leaves.

- Lilac-coloured flowers appear between April and November attracting bumblebees and honeybees. Weevils, beetles and caterpillars also feed on this vetch.

A NOTE OF ADVICE

The seeds can be eaten but they MUST be properly cooked in several changes of water before eating them. My advice is 'When in doubt, don't eat it!'

VETCH: COMMON

LATIN NAME: Vicia sativa

COMMON NAMES: Spring Vetch; Narrow-leaved Vetch; Poor Man's Peas

BEST TIME TO SEE: June - August

FLOWER COLOUR: Pink and mauve

HEIGHT/STEM LENGTH: 15 - 150cm

- This annual wildflower has spread into the wild after being grown for centuries as fodder for livestock. It was also used as green manure due to its ability to grow quickly and produce its own nitrates, making it a useful fertiliser. There is evidence that the Romans cultivated Vetch as an arable crop on farms, and harvested it to eat the foliage themselves.
- The Common Vetch has deep pink flowers in single or double clusters on long stalks, and hairy, yellowish seed pods. The seeds contain chemicals that could make them dangerous for animals, causing colic when eaten in quantity.

- Vetches spread with the help of animals, as the hard-shelled seeds survive in their digestive tracts and can spread a long way by this method.

A NOTE ON TOXICITY

The seeds of this vetch have been reported to contain small amounts of cyanide. My advice is 'When in doubt, don't eat it!'

VETCH: TUFTED

LATIN NAME: Vicia cracca.

COMMON NAMES: Cow Vetch; Bird Vetch; Blue Vetch; Boreal Vetch

BEST TIME TO SEE: June - August

FLOWER COLOUR: Purple and blue

HEIGHT/STEM LENGTH: 60 - 200cm

🌿 Tufted Vetch has a more exotic appearance than other Vetches. It flowers profusely, and its blooms make a real statement, with their pinky magenta buds maturing to purples and blues and growing in dense clusters along one side of the stem. Its curled tendrils, used for climbing and grasping, often spiral out from the ends. It can be seen along woodland edges, on scrub and grassland

🌿 Stronger than other vetch varieties, it will spread across whole hay fields, wobbly stems climbing towards the sunlight by supporting themselves on taller vegetation, sometimes ending in strangulation of the weaker species.

🌿 Tufted Vetch attracts a wide range of bees and butterflies as it is a good nectar source.

A NOTE OF ADVICE

The seeds can be eaten but they MUST be properly cooked in several changes of water before eating. My advice is 'When in doubt, don't eat it!'

VETCHLING: MEADOW

LATIN NAME: Lathyrus pratensis

SOME COMMON NAMES: Meadow Pea; Meadow Peavine

BEST TIME TO SEE: March - May

FLOWER COLOUR: Bright yellow

HEIGHT/STEM LENGTH: Up to 30cm

🌾 The yellow flowers of Meadow Vetchling, on their long stems, make a sunny show, often in big patches among the grasses at harvest time, or on a South facing sunny bank. With long tendrils, it climbs up other plants to get to the light.

🌾 Meadow Vetchling, with its sunny yellow flowers has a sad tale to tell - it has difficulty producing viable seeds. The seed pods don't develop on most of the flowers and the seeds are prone to being destroyed by hole-boring insects.

🌾 It is found on fertile soils in all sorts of grassy places such as meadows, pastures, hedges, road verges and railway banks.

🌾 The plant is reputed to repel mice!

A NOTE ON TOXICITY

Scientists suspect that the seeds of Yellow Vetchling may be dangerous to eat. Evidence is not conclusive, but my advice is 'When in doubt, don't eat it!'

WATER AVENS

LATIN NAME: Geum rivale

SOME COMMON NAMES: Avens Root, Chocolate Root, Cure All; Indian Chocolate

BEST TIME TO SEE: May - September

FLOWER COLOUR: Pink petals backed by purple or pink sepals

HEIGHT/STEM LENGTH: Up to 40cm

🌾 Water Avens has nodding, purple-and-orange flowers with five dark red sepals that surround orangey-pink petals and a cluster of yellow stamens. They hang on delicate, purple stems. Water Avens likes damp places, such as riversides, wet woodlands and damp meadows, but despite its name it is not aquatic.

🌾 The flowers appear from May to September and are followed by feathery seed heads. These have a distinct twist in the tail, as they can travel either by air using the feathers or by the kinked 'hook' getting caught in the fur of passing animals.

🌾 Big clumps of the plant attract dragonflies, bees and butterflies, which, in turn, bring hungry frogs, toads and other animals.

A FASCINATING FACT

The roots were once used as a chocolate substitute, giving it some of its common names such as Chocolate Root.

WILD GARLIC/RAMSONS

LATIN NAME: Allium ursinum

SOME COMMON NAMES: Bear Leek;
Bear's Garlic; Broad-Leaved Garlic;
Buckrams; Ramsons; Wood Garlic

BEST TIME TO SEE: April - June

FLOWER COLOUR: White

HEIGHT/STEM LENGTH: 45-50cm

🌿 The presence of this plant is a sign that the woodland you are walking in is very old. Wild Garlic, or Ramsons has green, pointed leaves and white flowers that reach out into starry bursts.

🌿 This bulbous perennial grows in dense clumps, often carpeting woodland floors and releasing an unmistakable scent of fresh, garlic. It prefers to grow in shady and damp conditions, and the wild garlic season often lasts all Spring.

🌿 It is used traditionally as a spring tonic due to its blood-purifying properties, similarly to bulb garlic. Its is also thought to lower cholesterol and blood-pressure, helping to reduce risk of heart attack or stroke.

🌿 The leaves can be eaten raw, cooked or blended to make a pesto to add to pasta, salads or soups.

A FASCINATING FACT

In Europe, the bulbs are thought to be a favourite food of brown bears, and the smell is said to deter cats.

WILLOWHERB: AMERICAN

LATIN NAME: Epilobium ciliatum

COMMON NAMES: Slender/
Fringed/Purple-leaved Willowherb

TIME TO SEE: June - August

FLOWER COLOUR: Pale pink, with
darker pink on backs of petals

HEIGHT/STEM LENGTH: 10 - 75cm

🌿 The dainty pink flowers of American
Willowherb, with deeply cut petals and reddish
stems with noticeable grooves, make a lovely
contribution to the countryside. It is a non-
native species of Willowherb, originating from
the USA, but now naturalised throughout the
UK.

🌿 Long, cylindrical and slightly hairy seedpods
pop open and curl back to reveal seeds with
white, fluffy hairs, which float away gently on
the wind to colonise other areas.

🌿 Like all willowherbs, American Willowherb does
not like shade and does best on more recently
disturbed land, such as
railway embankments
and the verges of new
roads, only yielding to
other plants over time.

A FASCINATING FACT

American Willowherb is widely used in the USA
cosmetic industry for creams, shampoos and baby
wipes.

WILLOWHERB: GREAT

LATIN NAME: Epilobium hirsutum.

COMMON NAMES: Apple Pie; Son-Before-the-Father; Codlins- and-Cream

BEST TIME TO SEE: June/August

FLOWER COLOUR: Deep magenta pink; creamy stamens

HEIGHT/STEM LENGTH: 80 - 180cm.

🌿 Great Willowherb is the largest native Willowherb found in the UK. It is tall, stately and covered in a fine down, with flowers of pinkish purple with paler centres, typically 2 to 3cm across. Petals are notched with frilly edges, thin, dark veins and large, creamy stamens in a central cross. The flower is sometimes called Son-before-the-Father, because the seed pods develop before the bright flowers open.

🌿 Great Willowherb is also sometimes known as 'Codlins-and-cream'. Codlins are cooking apples, so this name may have come from the rosy flowers with their creamy centres.

🌿 Great Willowherb is related to the yellow Evening Primrose, and enjoys damp places.

A NOTE ON TOXICITY

This plant could be toxic, and if eaten in quantity, it has been known to cause convulsions. My advice is 'When in doubt, don't eat it!'

WILLOWHERB: ROSEBAY

LATIN NAME: Chamerion angustifolium
COMMON NAMES: Fireweed; Blood Vine; Bombweed; Blooming Sally
TIME TO SEE: August/October
FLOWER COLOUR: Deep magenta pink; pink & white stamens
HEIGHT/STEM LENGTH: Up to 150cm

🌺 The bright magenta flower spikes of Rosebay Willowherb carpet roadsides, slopes and whole hillsides in late summer and early autumn. Favourite places are sunny slopes with plenty of light, good drainage and no competition. The seeds have fine silky hairs which help them to disperse over very long distances in the wind, establishing plants in new areas, where they can grow into big colonies.

🌺 Rosebay Willowherb is able to colonise untended land after fires and on bomb sites. This has given it names such as Fireweed or Bombweed. The heat from fires and bonfires can help to germinate them, hence another common name of 'Fireweed'.

A FASCINATING FACT

Each seed capsule splits and curls open, and inside are between 300 and 400 seeds. A single plant often yields an astonishing 80,000 seeds.

WOOD SAGE

LATIN NAME: Teucrium scorodonia

COMMON NAMES: Hind Heal; Wood Germander; Gypsy's Baccy

TIME TO SEE: June - August

FLOWER COLOUR: Pale greeny yellow; Centre - violet or red

HEIGHT/STEM LENGTH: 15 - 50cm

🌱 Wood Sage flowers are almost invisible with green spires above rough, downy, deeply textured leaves. It is a member of the Dead Nettle family, green all over, with tiny greeny-yellow flowers, each with four stamens with reddish or violet filaments, looking the same way from the stem.

🌱 Some people think the smell of crushed Wood Sage is like that of Sage, others say that it smells like Garlic, although it is not related to either. The leaves smell good when crushed, and taste like Hops. It is sometimes used to give beer a bitter taste as well as to clarify it and give the beer a rich hue.

🌱 Bees, wasps, beetles and butterflies all feed from Wood Sage; one beetle is even specific to it.

A FASCINATING FACT

Hind Heal is one name of this plant. It got this name from a belief in the country that deer eat this herb to heal snake bites.

WOOD SORREL

LATIN NAME: Oxalis acetosella

COMMON NAMES: Fairy Bells; Wood Sours; Cuckoo's Meat; Alleluia

TIME TO SEE: January - May

FLOWER COLOUR: White/sometimes pink; Centre - pale yellow

HEIGHT/STEM LENGTH: 5 - 15cm

🌿 Wood-sorrel blooms at Bluebell time, and the tiny white flowers light up the dark mossy banks. The flowers are white on the outside, often with tinges of pink inside, and pink or bright purple lines to lead insects to the nectar. Sometimes you will find whole groups with bright pink petals. It grows in places where the land has remained undisturbed for many years, so you will find it in old woodlands.

🌿 The delicate flowers and Shamrock-shaped leaves both close at night, when it rains, or if light levels become very low.

A FASCINATING FACT

Sorrel comes from the French for sour, and sorrel is a real thirst quencher on a walk in the woods. When chewed, the flavour of the leaves is like apple peel or lemon. It <u>is</u> safe to try!

WOOD SORREL: YELLOW

LATIN NAME: Oxalis corniculata atropupurea
COMMON NAMES: Common Yellow Wood Sorrel; Sleeping Beauty
TIME TO SEE: March - May
FLOWER COLOUR: Yellow; Centre - yellow
HEIGHT/STEM LENGTH: Up to 30cm

🌼 With bright yellow flowers and dark bronze-tinged leaves, this relative of the White Wood-sorrel has become widespread in the wild throughout the UK. Its origin is unknown, although it was introduced to Italy as a garden plant from South East Asia and spread here, where it flowers throughout the year. The leaves have a pronounced nick in the centre and are folded in the middle.

🌼 Yellow Wood-sorrel is good for home dyeing, producing yellow, orange and red/brown dyes from the flowers, or by boiling the plant with its roots to produce a natural yellow dye.

A FASCINATING FACT

When the leaves are chewed, a slimy substance forms in the mouth, and was used by magicians to protect their mouths when doing tricks involving eating glass.

WOUNDWORT: HEDGE

LATIN NAME: Stachys sylvatica

COMMON NAMES: Red Archangel; Allheal;
Hedge Nettle

TIME TO SEE: June - September

FLOWER COLOUR: Maroon and white; Centre -
white

HEIGHT/STEM LENGTH: 30 - 80cm

🌺 Woundwort, with deep green leaves and dark pinkish crimson flowers grows in the shady depths of field margins and hedgerows.

🌺 The hooded flowers have variegated lower lips, spotted white on the crimson background to tempt pollinators. The plant is related to the Dead Nettle, but smells rather unpleasant.

🌺 Bees and other insects love this plant and are frequent visitors to its maroon and purple flowers.

🌺 Woundwort is also said to repel midges and mosquitos if you make a salve from the leaves and rub it on your skin.

A FASCINATING FACT

Woundwort was used in the past to treat depression, and lift the spirits. In the future we may find out how it works!

YARROW

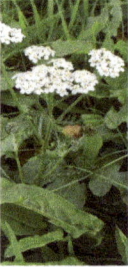

LATIN NAME: Achillea millefolium

COMMON NAMES: Nosebleed Plant; Thousand Leaf; Soldier's Woundwort

BEST TIME TO SEE: May – July

FLOWER COLOUR: Outer, ray petals - white; Inner florets - white

HEIGHT/STEM LENGTH: 8 - 50cm

🌿 Yarrow blooms in clusters of flat white flowers balanced on the tops of long stems with deeply cut leaves, as they stand tall among the summer grasses in fields and hedgerows. The plants often continue to flower well into the Autumn.

🌿 Yarrow is the pale country cousin of the popular garden flower Achillea, that we love to grow in summer borders.

🌿 Yarrow has long roots that access minerals from deep in the soil and these benefit the animals when they eat the plants in winter hay fodder. This makes it a welcome addition to traditional hay meadows.

A FASCINATING FACT

Chamazulene Blue, a dark blue essential oil can be distilled from the flowers of Yarrow, and is used in skin oils and rubs to combat chest problems.

YELLOW RATTLE

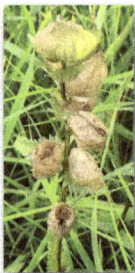

LATIN NAME: Rhinanthus minor

COMMON NAMES: Cockscomb; Penny Grass; Hay Rattle

BEST TIME TO SEE: March – July

FLOWER COLOUR: Bright yellow with dark red spots; Centre – yellow

HEIGHT/STEM LENGTH: Up to 50cm

🌾 The yellow flowers of Yellow Rattle, spotted with red or russet, and the signature papery, rattling seed heads give this flower the two parts of its name. Rattle is a plant parasite, which weakens grasses, reducing their strength by as much as 50%, and allowing wildflowers to invade the resulting spaces.

🌾 The final flower in this collection is one of the most important in traditional haymaking, and Yellow Rattle is one reason why we can still have meadows rich in wildflowers.

🌾 Yellow Rattle does a great service to biodiversity, and should be treasured, planted widely, and encouraged to spread.

A FASCINATING FACT

As Yellow Rattle seeds ripen, the seed vessels rattle loudly as they wave in the wind among the hay at harvest time, spreading their seeds across the fields.

There are laws protecting wild flowers.

🌷 you must not pick flowers in a conservation area, or cultivated flowers in your local park or city centre.

🌷 you must NOT uproot any wild plant.

🌷 Bluebells are protected and must NOT be picked or disturbed at any time.

The 'free to pick' list:

Many children's dictionaries have now removed the names of common flowers and trees from their latest editions. Plantlife www.plantlife.org.uk has published a list of 12 wildflowers that children should be encouraged to pick, so they learn the names of the most common flowers that are becoming lost to their language.

Please feel free to encourage young children to pick these flowers!

1. Daisy*
2. Primrose
3. Greater Stitchwort*
4. Meadow Buttercup*
5. Oxeye Daisy*
6. Common Knapweed*

7. Dandelion*
8. Dog Violet
9. Cow Parsley*
10. Red Campion
11. Yarrow*
12. Meadowsweet*

*Flowers with a * are identified in this book.*

Remember the Plantlife rules when picking any of the 12 'free to pick' wild flowers:

1. Don't trespass on private land.

2. Never pick flowers from nature reserves or any other protected sites.

3. Only pick from large patches of flowers; leave plenty of flowers for others, to set seed, and for pollen, nectar, seed or shelter for other wildlife.

4. Only pick one flower of every twenty you find. Never diminish the display. Remember others coming after you.

5. Only pick a small handful of flowers for personal use, never for commercial gain.

6. Don't trample other flowers or vegetation.

7. Never uproot any plant unless you have the landowner's permission.

8. If in doubt, don't pick. If you don't know what the plant is, leave it where it is. Take a photograph instead and try to identify it when you get home.

Remember: Once picked, wildflowers don't last, even in water, so leave them where you find them.

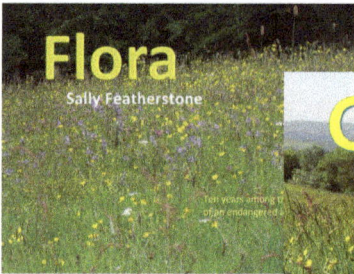

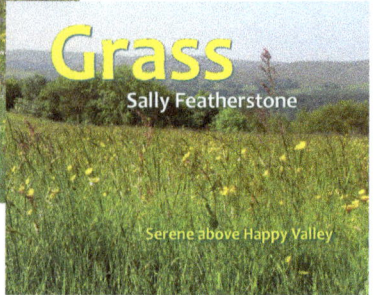

For ten years I had the privilege of living in the middle of hay meadows in West Yorkshire. These seven fields are a precious few of the last natural hay fields remaining in the UK, their destruction the result of our hunger for increased agricultural productivity. Out of this experience have come two books, each illustrated with colour photos on every page.

Flora celebrates in detail the hundred wild flowers that grow in these fields, and *Grass* describes the progress of the year in traditionally managed upland hay meadows. As the land responds to the seasons, and the animals and humans contribute to the production of the grass, watch the growth and production of the hay that feeds the farms through the winter.

Flora - ten years among the flowers of an endangered landscape 9781999332440 *Grass* - serene above Happy Valley 9781739350727